NATIONAL GANG INTELLIGENCE CENTER

2011

NATIONAL GANG THREAT ASSESSMENT
Emerging Trends

2011

NATIONAL GANG THREAT ASSESSMENT
Emerging Trends

ISBN 978-1-61448-154-6 Paperback

ISBN 978-1-61448-155-3 eBook

SPECIAL THANKS TO THE NATIONAL DRUG INTELLIGENCE CENTER
FOR THEIR CONTRIBUTIONS AND SUPPORT.

2011 National Gang Threat Assessment – Emerging Trends

Preface

The National Gang Intelligence Center (NGIC) prepared the 2011 National Gang Threat Assessment (NGTA) to examine emerging gang trends and threats posed by criminal gangs to communities throughout the United States. The 2011 NGTA enhances and builds on the gang-related trends and criminal threats identified in the 2009 assessment. It supports US Department of Justice strategic objectives 2.2 (to reduce the threat, incidence, and prevalence of violent crime) and 2.4 (to reduce the threat, trafficking, use, and related violence of illegal drugs). The assessment is based on federal, state, local, and tribal law enforcement and corrections agency intelligence, including information and data provided by the National Drug Intelligence Center (NDIC) and the National Gang Center. Additionally, this assessment is supplemented by information retrieved from open source documents and data collected through April 2011.

Scope and Methodology

In 2009, the NGIC released its second threat assessment on gang activity in the United States. The NGIC and its law enforcement partners documented increases in gang proliferation and migration nationwide and emerging threats. This report attempts to expand on these findings. Reporting and intelligence collected over the past two years have demonstrated increases in the number of gangs and gang members as law enforcement authorities nationwide continue to identify gang members and share information regarding these groups. Better reporting and collection has contributed greatly to the increased documentation and reporting of gang members and gang trends.

Information in the 2011 National Gang Threat Assessment-Emerging Trends was derived from law enforcement intelligence, open source information, and data collected from the NDIC, including the 2010 NDIC National Drug Threat Survey (NDTS). NGIC law enforcement partners provided information and guidance regarding new trends and intelligence through an online request for information via the NGIC Law Enforcement Online (LEO) Special Interest Group (SIG), which is now NGIC Online. Law enforcement agencies nationwide continuously report new and emerging gang trends to the NGIC, as the NGIC continues to operate as a repository and dissemination hub for gang intelligence. This information provided by our law enforcement partners was used to identify many of the trends and issues included in this report.

Reporting used to quantify the number of street and outlaw motorcycle gangs and gang members was primarily derived from the 2010 NDIC NDTS data and some supplemental NGIC reporting from our law enforcement partners. NDIC annually conducts the NDTS to collect data on the threat posed by various illicit drugs in the United States. A stratified random sample of nearly 3,500 state and local law enforcement agencies was surveyed to generate national, regional, and state estimates of various aspects of drug trafficking activities including the threat posed by various drugs, the availability and production of illicit drugs, as well as the role of street gangs and outlaw motorcycle gangs in drug trafficking activity. Weighted national, regional, and state-level statistical estimates derived from NDTS 2010 data was based on responses received from 2,963 law enforcement agencies out of a sample of 3,465 agencies. In calculating the number of street and outlaw motorcycle gang members, respondents in each region were asked to select from a series of ranges of numbers. The median numbers of each range were aggregated to generate an estimate for the total number of gang members. In calculating the number of street and outlaw motorcycle gangs, the low end of each range was aggregated to generate an estimate for the total number of gangs and gang members. Prison gang member estimates were derived directly from the US Federal Bureau of Prisons (BOP) and state correctional institutions across the country.

About the NGIC

The NGIC was established by Congress in 2005 to support law enforcement agencies through timely and accurate information sharing and strategic/tactical analysis of federal, state, and local law enforcement information focusing on the growth, migration, criminal activity, and association of gangs that pose a significant threat to communities throughout the United States. The NGIC is comprised of representatives from the Federal Bureau of Investigation (FBI), US Drug Enforcement Administration (DEA), US Bureau of Alcohol, Tobacco, Firearms, and Explosives (ATF), US Bureau of Prisons (BOP), United States Marshals Service (USMS), US Immigration and Customs Enforcement (ICE), US Department of Defense (DOD), National Drug Intelligence Center (NDIC), and US Customs and Border Protection (CBP). This multi-agency fusion center integrates gang intelligence assets to serve as a central intelligence resource for gang information and analytical support.

To assist in the sharing of gang intelligence with law enforcement, the NGIC has established NGIC Online, an information system comprised of a set of web-based tools designed for researching gang-related intelligence and sharing of information with federal, state, local and tribal law enforcement partners. The system's Request for Information (RFI) portal encourages users to contribute new data as well as conduct gang research through custom threat assessments and/or liaison with NGIC's network of national subject matter experts. NGIC Online functions include RFI submissions and responses; Gang Encyclopedia WIKI; General Intelligence Library; and a Signs, Symbols, and Tattoos (SST) database with user submissions.

Gang Definitions

GANG	DEFINITION
Street	Street gangs are criminal organizations formed on the street operating throughout the United States.
Prison	Prison gangs are criminal organizations that originated within the penal system and operate within correctional facilities throughout the United States, although released members may be operating on the street. Prison gangs are also self-perpetuating criminal entities that can continue their criminal operations outside the confines of the penal system.
Outlaw Motorcycle (OMGs)	OMGs are organizations whose members use their motorcycle clubs as conduits for criminal enterprises. Although some law enforcement agencies regard only One Percenters as OMGs, the NGIC, for the purpose of this assessment, covers all OMG criminal organizations, including OMG support and puppet clubs.
One Percenter OMGs	ATF defines *One Percenters* as any group of motorcyclists who have voluntarily made a commitment to band together to abide by their organization's rules enforced by violence and who engage in activities that bring them and their club into repeated and serious conflict with society and the law. The group must be an ongoing organization, association of three (3) or more persons which have a common interest and/or activity characterized by the commission of or involvement in a pattern of criminal or delinquent conduct. ATF estimates there are approximately 300 One Percenter OMGs in the United States.
Neighborhood/Local	Neighborhood or Local street gangs are confined to specific neighborhoods and jurisdictions and often imitate larger, more powerful national gangs. The primary purpose for many neighborhood gangs is drug distribution and sales.

Regional Breakdown:

Maps and data in this assessment are presented according to the FBI's Safe Streets Gang Task Force regions.

REGION	STATES
North Central	Illinois, Indiana, Iowa, Kansas, Kentucky, Michigan, Minnesota, Missouri, Nebraska, North Dakota, Ohio, South Dakota, Wisconsin
Northeast	Connecticut, Maine, Massachusetts, New Hampshire, New Jersey, New York, Pennsylvania, Rhode Island, Vermont, West Virginia
South Central	Alabama, Arkansas, Louisiana, Mississippi, Oklahoma, Tennessee, Texas
Southeast	Delaware, District of Columbia, Florida, Georgia, Maryland, North Carolina, Puerto Rico, South Carolina, Virginia
West	Alaska, Arizona, California, Colorado, Hawaii, Idaho, Montana, Nevada, New Mexico, Oregon, Utah, Washington, Wyoming

Executive Summary

Gangs continue to commit criminal activity, recruit new members in urban, suburban, and rural regions across the United States, and develop criminal associations that expand their influence over criminal enterprises, particularly street-level drug sales. The most notable trends for 2011 have been the overall increase in gang membership, and the expansion of criminal street gangs' control of street-level drug sales and collaboration with rival gangs and other criminal organizations.[a]

Key Findings

Gangs are expanding, evolving and posing an increasing threat to US communities nationwide. Many gangs are sophisticated criminal networks with members who are violent, distribute wholesale quantities of drugs, and develop and maintain close working relationships with members and associates of transnational criminal/drug trafficking organizations. Gangs are becoming more violent while engaging in less typical and lower-risk crime, such as prostitution and white-collar crime. Gangs are more adaptable, organized, sophisticated, and opportunistic, exploiting new and advanced technology as a means to recruit, communicate discretely, target their rivals, and perpetuate their criminal activity. Based on state, local, and federal law enforcement reporting, the NGIC concludes that:

---

[a] **Title 18 U.S.C. Section 521(a)(A)** defines criminal street gangs as ongoing groups, clubs, organizations, or associations of five or more individuals that have as one of their primary purposes the commission of one or more criminal offenses. Title 18 U.S.C. Section 521(c) further defines such criminal offenses as (1) a federal felony involving a controlled substance; (2) a federal felony crime of violence that has as an element the use or attempted use of physical force against the person of another and (3) a conspiracy to commit an offense described in paragraph (1) or (2).

- There are approximately 1.4 million active street, prison, and OMG gang members comprising more than 33,000 gangs in the United States. Gang membership increased most significantly in the Northeast and Southeast regions, although the West and Great Lakes regions boast the highest number of gang members. Neighborhood-based gangs, hybrid gang members, and national-level gangs such as the Sureños are rapidly expanding in many jurisdictions. Many communities are also experiencing an increase in ethnic-based gangs such as African, Asian, Caribbean, and Eurasian gangs.

- Gangs are responsible for an average of 48 percent of violent crime in most jurisdictions and up to 90 percent in several others, according to NGIC analysis. Major cities and suburban areas experience the most gang-related violence. Local neighborhood-based gangs and drug crews continue to pose the most significant criminal threat in most communities. Aggressive recruitment of juveniles and immigrants, alliances and conflict between gangs, the release of incarcerated gang members from prison, advancements in technology and communication, and Mexican Drug Trafficking Organization (MDTO) involvement in drug distribution have resulted in gang expansion and violence in a number of jurisdictions.

- Gangs are increasingly engaging in non-traditional gang-related crime, such as alien smuggling, human trafficking, and prostitution. Gangs are also engaging in white collar crime such as counterfeiting, identity theft, and mortgage fraud, primarily due to the high profitability and much lower visibility and risk of detection and punishment than drug and weapons trafficking.

- US-based gangs have established strong working relationships with Central American and MDTOs to perpetrate illicit cross-border activity, as well as with some organized crime groups in some regions of the United States. US-based gangs and MDTOs are establishing wide-reaching drug networks; assisting in the smuggling of drugs, weapons, and illegal immigrants along the Southwest Border; and serving as enforcers for MDTO interests on the US side of the border.

- Many gang members continue to engage in gang activity while incarcerated. Family members play pivotal roles in assisting or facilitating gang activities and recruitment during a gang members' incarceration. Gang members in some correctional facilities are adopting radical religious views while incarcerated.

- Gangs encourage members, associates, and relatives to obtain law enforcement, judiciary, or legal employment in order to gather information on rival gangs and law enforcement operations. Gang infiltration of the military continues to pose a significant criminal threat, as members of at least 53 gangs have been identified on both domestic and international military installations. Gang members who learn advanced weaponry and combat techniques in the military are at risk of employing these skills on the street when they return to their communities.

- Gang members are acquiring high-powered, military-style weapons and equipment which poses a significant threat because of the potential to engage in lethal encounters with law enforcement officers and civilians. Typically firearms are acquired through illegal purchases; straw purchases via surrogates or middle-men, and thefts from individuals, vehicles, residences and commercial establishments. Gang members also target military and law enforcement officials, facilities, and vehicles to obtain weapons, ammunition, body armor, police gear, badges, uniforms, and official identification.

- Gangs on Indian Reservations often emulate national-level gangs and adopt names and identifiers from nationally recognized urban gangs. Gang members on some Indian Reservations are associating with gang members in the community to commit crime.

- Gangs are becoming increasingly adaptable and sophisticated, employing new and advanced technology to facilitate criminal activity discreetly, enhance their criminal operations, and connect with other gang members, criminal organizations, and potential recruits nationwide and even worldwide.

Current Gang-Related Trends and Crime

Gang membership continues to expand throughout communities nationwide, as gangs evolve, adapt to new threats, and form new associations. Consequently, gang-related crime and violence is increasing as gangs employ violence and intimidation to control their territory and illicit operations. Many gangs have advanced beyond their traditional role as local retail drug distributors in large cities to become more organized, adaptable, and influential in large-scale drug trafficking. Gang members are migrating from urban areas to suburban and rural communities to recruit new members, expand their drug distribution territories, form new alliances, and collaborate with rival gangs and criminal organizations for profit and influence. Local neighborhood, hybrid and female gang membership is on the rise in many communities. Prison gang members, who exert control over many street gang members, often engage in crime and violence upon their return to the community. Gang members returning to the community from prison have an adverse and lasting impact on neighborhoods, which may experience notable increases in crime, violence, and drug trafficking.

GANG MEMBERSHIP AND EXPANSION

Approximately 1.4 million active street, OMG, and prison gang members, comprising more than 33,000 gangs, are criminally active within all 50 US states, the District of Columbia, and Puerto Rico (see Appendix A). This represents a 40 percent increase from an estimated 1 million gang members in 2009. The NGIC attributes this increase in gang membership primarily to improved reporting, more aggressive recruitment efforts by gangs, the formation of new gangs, new opportunities for drug trafficking, and collaboration with rival gangs and drug trafficking organizations (DTOs). Law enforcement in several jurisdictions also attribute the increase in gang membership in their region to the gangster rap culture, the facilitation of communication and recruitment through the Internet and social media, the proliferation of generational gang members, and a shortage of resources to combat gangs.

More than half of NGIC law enforcement partners report an increase in gang-related criminal activity in their jurisdictions over the past two years. Neighborhood-based gangs continue to pose the greatest threat in most jurisdictions nationwide.

- NGIC and NDIC data indicates that, since 2009, gang membership increased most significantly in the Northeast and Southeast regions, although the West and North Central regions—particularly Arizona, California, and Illinois—boast the highest number of gang members.

2011 Estimated Gang Membership		
	MEMBERS	GANGS
Street	1,140,344	30,313
OMG	44,108	2,965
Prison	231,136**	n/a
Total	1,415,578	33,278

*Based on 2010 and 2011 NGIC and NDIC data
**Based on reporting from 32 states

2011 Estimated Street and OMG Membership by Region	
North Central	260,022
Northeast	159,158
South Central	167,353
Southeast	117,205
West	480,715
Total	1,184,453

*Based on 2010 and 2011 NGIC and NDIC data

- Sureño gangs, including Mara Salvatrucha (MS-13), 18th Street, and Florencia 13, are expanding faster than other national-level gangs, both in membership and geographically. Twenty states and the District of Columbia report an increase of Sureño migration into their region over the past three years. California has experienced a substantial migration of Sureño gangs into northern California and neighboring states, such as Arizona, Nevada, and Oregon.

- Law enforcement reporting indicates a significant increase in OMGs in a number of jurisdictions, with 44,108 members nationwide comprising approximately 2,965 gangs.[b] Jurisdictions in Alaska, Arizona, Colorado, Connecticut, Delaware, Florida, Georgia, Iowa, Missouri, Montana, Oregon, Pennsylvania, South Carolina, Tennessee, Utah, and Virginia are experiencing the most significant increase in OMGs, increasing the potential for gang-related turf wars with other local OMGs. The Wheels of Soul (WOS), Mongols, Outlaws, Pagans and Vagos have expanded in several states.

---

[b] For the purpose of this assessment, OMGs include One Percenter gangs as well as support and puppet clubs.

Table 1. Recent Expansion of Major OMGs:

GANG	REGION
Mongols	Arizona, Arkansas, California, Colorado, Illinois, Kentucky, Montana, Nevada, New York, Oklahoma, Oregon, Washington
Outlaws	Arkansas, Montana, Maryland, North Carolina, New York
Pagans	Delaware, New Jersey, Ohio
Vagos	California, Florida, Georgia, Mississippi, Nevada, New Mexico, New York, Oregon, Pennsylvania, Rhode Island, South Dakota
Wheels of Soul	Alabama, Arkansas, California, Colorado, Illinois, Kentucky, New York

Source: ATF

Figure 1. Nationwide Gang Presence

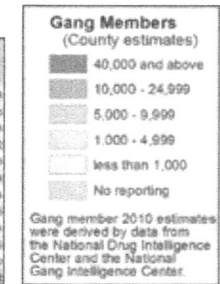

Source: NGIC and NDIC 2010 National Drug Survey Data

Chart 1. Threat Posed by Gangs, According to Law Enforcement.
The NGIC collected intelligence from law enforcement officials nationwide in an attempt to capture the threat posed by national-level street, prison, outlaw motorcycle, and neighborhood-based gangs in their communities.

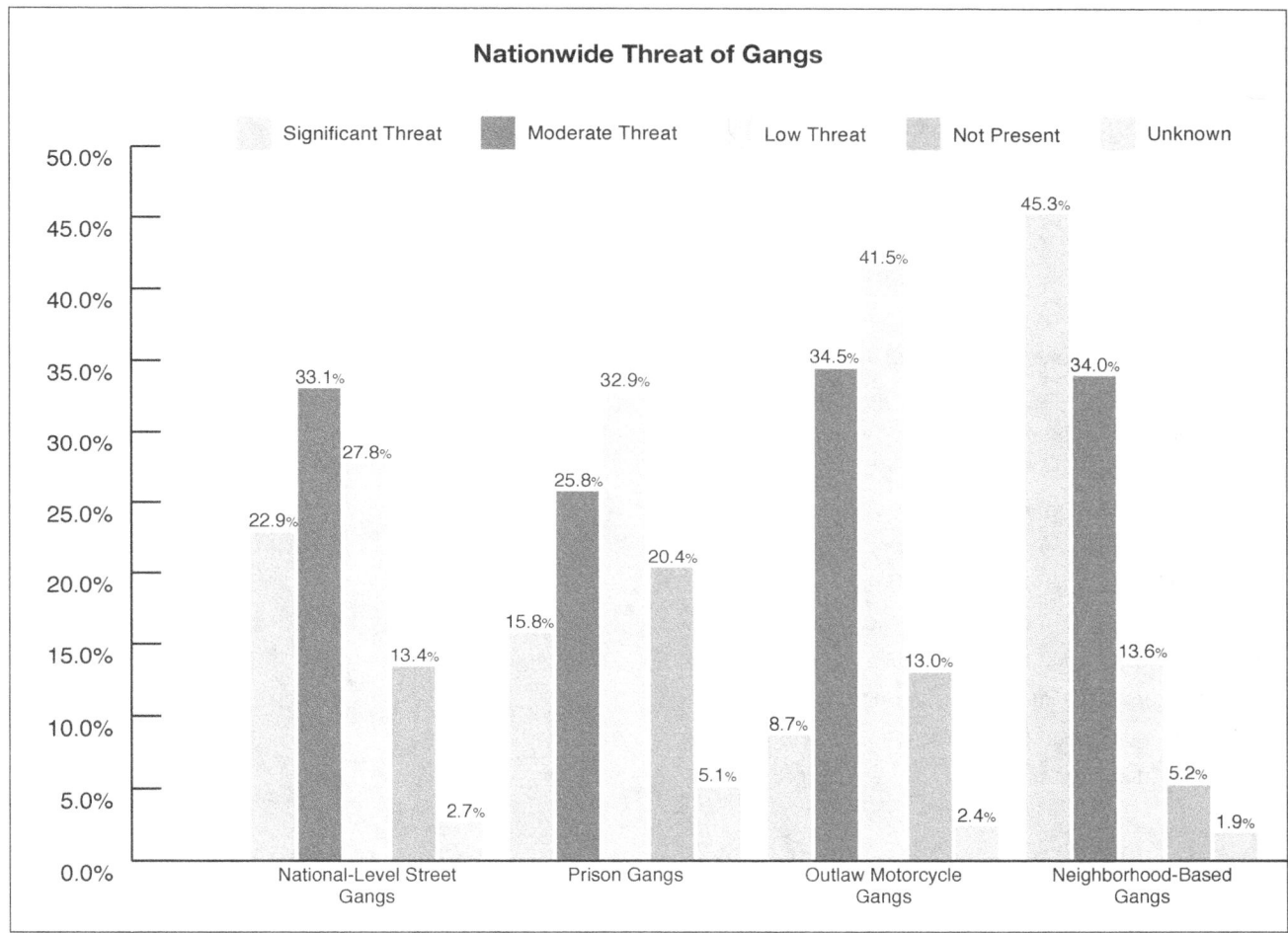

Source: 2011 NGIC National data

GANG-RELATED VIOLENT CRIME

Gang-related crime and violence continues to rise. NGIC analysis indicates that gang members are responsible for an average of 48 percent of violent crime in most jurisdictions and much higher in others. Some jurisdictions in Arizona, California, Colorado, Illinois, Massachusetts, Oklahoma, and Texas report that gangs are responsible for at least 90 percent of crime. A comparison of FBI Uniform Crime Reporting (UCR) 2009 violent crime data and 2010 NGIC gang data illustrates that regions experiencing the most violent crime—including southern California, Texas, and Florida—also have a substantial gang presence (see Figure 1 and Map 7). Street gangs are involved in a host of violent criminal activities, including assault, drug trafficking, extortion, firearms offenses, home invasion robberies, homicide, intimidation, shootings, and weapons trafficking. NDIC reporting indicates that gang control over drug distribution and disputes over drug territory has increased, which may be responsible for the increase in violence in many areas. Conflict between gangs, gang migration into rival gang territory, and the release of incarcerated gang members back into the community has also resulted in an increase in gang-related crime and violence in many jurisdictions, according to NGIC reporting.

Table 2. Percentage of Violent Crime Committed by Gangs as reported by NGIC Law Enforcement Partners

% OF VIOLENT CRIME COMMITTED BY GANGS	% OF LE OFFICIALS
1-25%	34.0%
26-50%	28.4%
51-75%	22.7%
76-100%	14.9%

Chart 2. Threat Posed by Gangs, as Reported by Law Enforcement.
The NGIC collected intelligence from its law enforcement partners nationwide in an effort to capture the criminal threat posed by national-level street, prison, outlaw motorcycle, and neighborhood-based gangs in their communities. The following chart represents the percentage of gang involvement in crime.

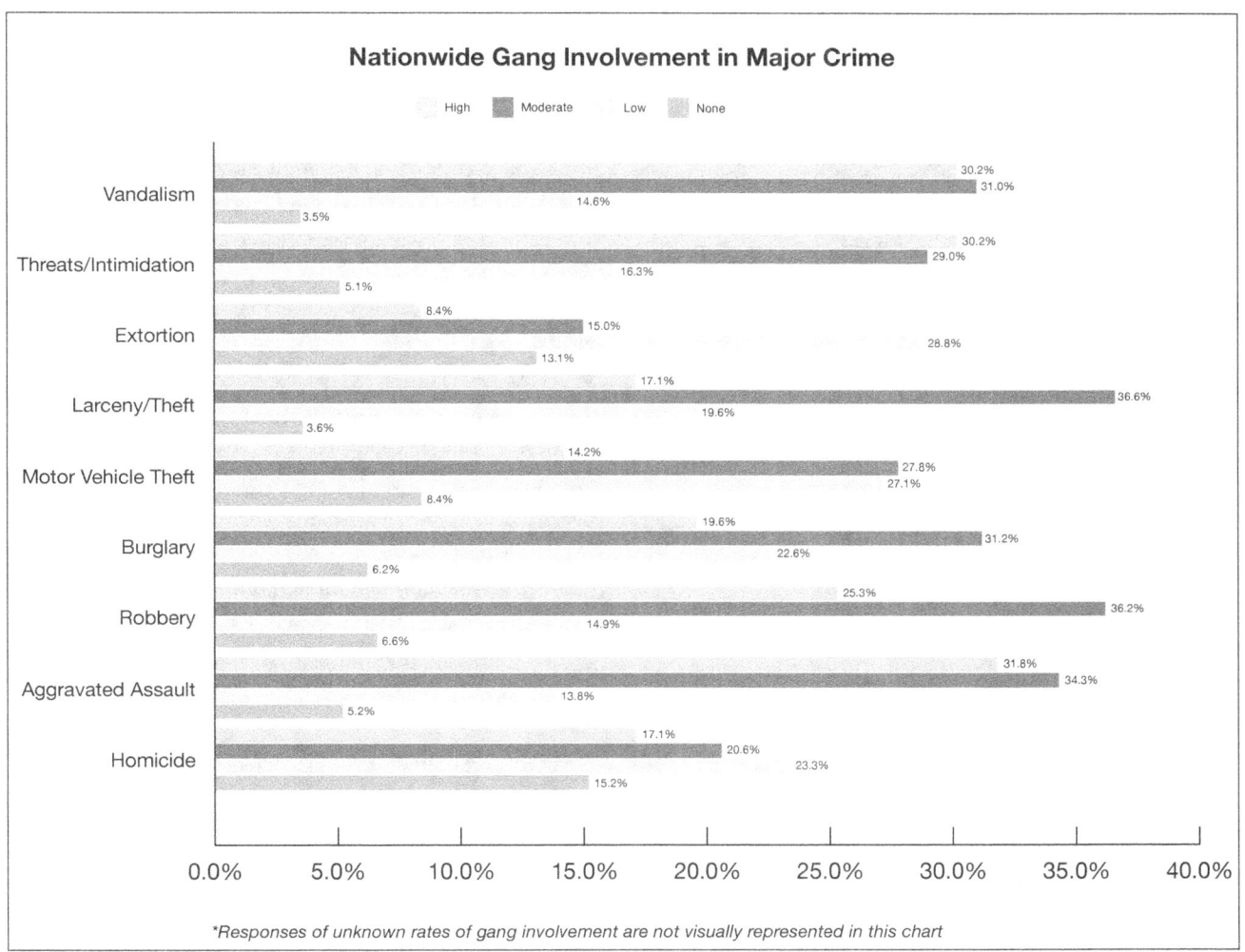

Nationwide Gang Involvement in Major Crime

Legend: High, Moderate, Low, None

Crime	High	Moderate	Low	None
Vandalism	30.2%	31.0%	14.6%	3.5%
Threats/Intimidation	30.2%	29.0%	16.3%	5.1%
Extortion	8.4%	15.0%	28.8%	13.1%
Larceny/Theft	17.1%	36.6%	19.6%	3.6%
Motor Vehicle Theft	14.2%	27.8%	27.1%	8.4%
Burglary	19.6%	31.2%	22.6%	6.2%
Robbery	25.3%	36.2%	14.9%	6.6%
Aggravated Assault	31.8%	34.3%	13.8%	5.2%
Homicide	17.1%	20.6%	23.3%	15.2%

0.0% 5.0% 10.0% 15.0% 20.0% 25.0% 30.0% 35.0% 40.0%

*Responses of unknown rates of gang involvement are not visually represented in this chart

Source: 2011 NGIC data

According to National Youth Gang Survey reporting, larger cities and suburban counties accounted for the majority of gang-related violence and more than 96 percent of all gang homicides in 2009.[1] As previous studies have indicated, neighborhood-based gangs and drug crews continue to pose the most significant criminal threat in these regions.

- Law enforcement officials in the Washington, DC metropolitan region are concerned about a spate of gang-related violence in their area. In February 2011, ICE officials indicted 11 MS-13 members for a two-year spree of murders, stabbings, assaults, robberies, and drug distribution. Likewise, gangs such as MS-13 and Bloods in Prince George's County, Maryland, are suspected to be involved in up to 16 homicides since January 2011.[2]

- USMS reported 5,705 gang-affiliated felony fugitives in 2010, a 14 percent increase from the number of gang fugitives in 2009. California and Texas report the highest number of gang fugitives, with 1,284 and 542 respectively.

GANG-RELATED DRUG DISTRIBUTION AND TRAFFICKING

Gang involvement and control of the retail drug trade poses a serious threat to public safety and stability in most major cities and in many mid-size cities because such distribution activities are routinely associated with lethal violence. Violent disputes over control of drug territory and enforcement of drug debts frequently occur among gangs in both urban and suburban areas, as gangs expand their control of drug distribution in many jurisdictions, according to NDIC and NGIC reporting. In 2010, law enforcement agencies in 51 major US cities reported moderate to significant levels of gang-related drug activity.

NDIC survey data indicates that 69 percent of US law enforcement agencies report gang involvement in drug distribution.

- In June 2010, a joint federal-state law enforcement operation led to the arrest of eight people linked to a San Gabriel Valley street gang involved in violent crimes and methamphetamine trafficking in support of the California Mexican Mafia (La Eme).[3]

NDIC reporting suggests that gangs are advancing beyond their traditional role as local retail drug distributors in large cities and becoming more influential in large-scale drug trafficking, resulting in an increase in violent crime in several regions of the country.[4]

- Law enforcement reporting indicates that gang-related drug distribution and trafficking has resulted in an increase of kidnappings, assaults, robberies and homicides along the US Southwest border region.

Gang involvement in drug trafficking has also resulted in the expansion and migration of some gangs into new US communities, according to NDIC reporting.

- Gang members from the Midwest are migrating to southern states to expand their drug trafficking operations.

Figure 3. Major Cities Reporting Gang-Related Drug Activity in 2010

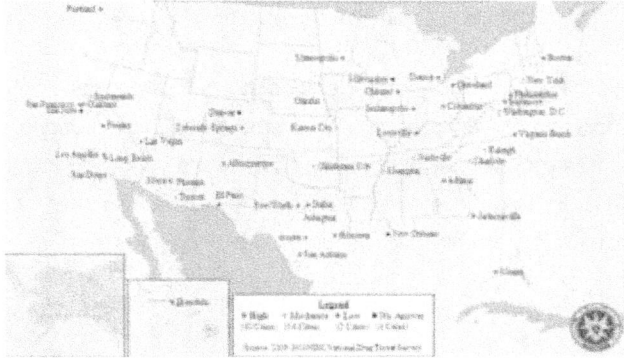

Source: NDIC 2010 National Drug Threat Survey

JUVENILE GANGS

Many jurisdictions are experiencing an increase in juvenile gangs[c] and violence, which is often attributed, in part, to the increased incarceration rates of older members and the aggressive recruitment of juveniles in schools. Gangs have traditionally targeted youths because of their vulnerability and susceptibility to recruitment tactics, as well as their likelihood of avoiding harsh criminal sentencing and willingness to engage in violence.

NGIC reporting indicates that juvenile gangs are responsible for a majority of crime in various jurisdictions in Arizona, California, Connecticut, Florida, Georgia, Illinois, Maryland, Michigan, Missouri, North Carolina, New Hampshire, South Carolina, Texas, Virginia, and Washington.

- Juvenile gang members in some communities are hosting parties and organizing special events which develop into opportunities for recruiting, drugs, sexual exploitation, and criminal activity.

[c] A juvenile refers to an individual under 18 years of age, although in some states, a juvenile refers to an individual under 16 years of age. A juvenile gang refers to a gang that is primarily comprised of individuals under 18 years of age.

- Gangster Rap gangs, often comprised of juveniles, are forming and are being used to launder drug money through seemingly legitimate businesses, according to NGIC reporting.

GANG ALLIANCES AND COLLABORATION

Collaboration between rival gangs and criminal organizations and increased improvement in communications, transportation, and technology have enabled national-level gangs to expand and secure their criminal networks throughout the United States and in other countries.

- According to NGIC reporting, gang members in California are collaborating with members of rival gangs to further criminal activities such as drug distribution, prostitution of minors, and money laundering.

- Gangs in the correctional system are committing crimes for other gangs in an effort to confuse and evade law enforcement.

GANG SOPHISTICATION

Gang members are becoming more sophisticated in their structure and operations and are modifying their activity to minimize law enforcement scrutiny and circumvent gang enhancement laws. Gangs in several jurisdictions have modified or ceased traditional or stereotypical gang indicia and no longer display their colors, tattoos, or hand signs. Others are forming hybrid gangs to avoid police attention and make to it more difficult for law enforcement to identify and monitor them, according to NGIC reporting. Many gangs are engaging in more sophisticated criminal schemes, including white collar and cyber crime, targeting and infiltrating sensitive systems to gain access to sensitive areas or information, and targeting and monitoring law enforcement.

Expansion of Ethnic-Based and Non-Traditional Gangs

Law enforcement officials in jurisdictions nationwide report an expansion of African, Asian, Eurasian, Caribbean, and Middle Eastern gangs, according to NGIC reporting. Many communities are also experiencing increases in hybrid and non-traditional gangs.

ASIAN GANGS

Asian gangs, historically limited to regions with large Asian populations, are expanding throughout communities nationwide. Although often considered street gangs, Asian gangs operate similar to Asian Criminal Enterprises with a more structured organization and hierarchy. They are not turf-oriented like most African-American and Hispanic street gangs and typically maintain a low profile to avoid law enforcement scrutiny. Asian gang members are known to prey on their own race and often develop a relationship with their victims before victimizing them.[5] Law enforcement officials have limited knowledge of Asian gangs and often have difficulty penetrating these gangs because of language barriers and gang distrust of non-Asians.[6]

Law enforcement officials in California, Georgia, Maryland, Massachusetts, Michigan, Montana, Pennsylvania, Rhode Island, Virginia, and Wisconsin report a significant increase in Asian gangs in their jurisdictions.

Asian gangs are involved in a host of criminal activities to include violent crime, drug and human trafficking, and white collar crime.

- Asian gang members in New England and California maintain marijuana cultivation houses specifically for the manufacturing and distribution of high potency marijuana and pay members of the Asian community to reside in them, according to 2010 NDIC and open source reporting.[7]

Some law enforcement agencies attribute the recent increase in Asian gang membership in their jurisdictions to the recruitment of non-Asian members into the gang in order to compete more effectively with other street gangs for territory and dominance of illicit markets.

EAST AFRICAN GANGS

Somali Gangs

Somali gang presence has increased in several cities throughout the United States. Somali gangs are most prevalent in the Minneapolis-St. Paul, Minnesota; San Diego, California; and Seattle, Washington areas, primarily as a result of proximity to the Mexican and Canadian borders, according to ICE, NGIC, and law enforcement reporting. Somali gang activity has also been reported in other cities throughout the United States such as Nashville, Tennessee; Clarkston, Georgia; Columbus, Ohio; East Brunswick, New Jersey; and Tucson, Arizona. Unlike most traditional street gangs, Somali gangs tend to align and adopt gang names based on clan or tribe, although a few have joined national gangs such as the Crips and Bloods.

NGIC reporting indicates that East African gangs are present in at least 30 jurisdictions, including those in California, Georgia, Minnesota, Ohio, Texas, Virginia, and Washington.

Somalian gangs are involved in drug and weapons trafficking, human trafficking, credit card fraud, prostitution, and violent crime. Homicides involving Somali victims are often the result of clan feuds between gang members. Sex trafficking of females across jurisdictional and state

Figure 4. Somali Outlaws set in Minneapolis, MN

Source: Minneapolis Police Department

borders for the purpose of prostitution is also a growing trend among Somalian gangs.

- In November 2010, 29 suspected Somalian gang members were indicted for a prostitution trafficking operation, according to open source reporting. Over a 10 year period, Somalian gang members transported underage females from Minnesota to Ohio and Tennessee for prostitution.[8]

- In February 2009, five Somali gang members were arrested for murdering drug dealers in Dexter and Athens, Ohio, during home invasion robberies, according to law enforcement reporting.[9]

Although some Somali gangs adopt Bloods or Crips gang monikers, they typically do not associate with other African-American gangs. Somali nationals—mostly refugees displaced by the war(s) in Somalia and surrounding countries—tend to migrate to specific low-income communities, which are often heavily controlled by local Bloods and Crips street gangs. The Somali youth may emulate the local gangs, which frequently leads to friction with other gangs, such as Bloods and Crips, as well as with Ethiopian gangs.

Sudanese Gangs

Sudanese gangs in the United States have been expanding since 2003 and have been reported in Iowa, Minnesota, Nebraska, North Dakota, South Dakota, and Tennessee. Some Sudanese gang members have weapons and tactical knowledge from their involvement in conflicts in their native country.

- The African Pride (AP) gang is one of the most aggressive and dangerous of the Sudanese street gangs in Iowa, Minnesota, Nebraska, and North and South Dakota.

CARIBBEAN GANGS

Although largely confined to the East Coast, Caribbean gangs, such as Dominican, Haitian, and Jamaican gangs, are expanding in a number of communities throughout the United States.

Dominican Gangs

The Trinitarios, the most rapidly-expanding Caribbean gang and the largest Dominican gang, are a violent prison gang with members operating on the street. The Trinitarios are involved in homicide, violent assaults, robbery, theft, home invasions, and street-level drug distribution. Although predominate in New York and New Jersey, the Trinitarios have expanded to communities throughout the eastern United States, including Georgia, Massachusetts, Pennsylvania, and Rhode Island. Dominicans Don't Play (DDP), the second largest Dominican gang based in Bronx, New York, are known for their violent machete attacks and drug trafficking activities in Florida, Michigan, New Jersey, New York, and Pennsylvania.

An increase in the Dominican population in several eastern US jurisdictions has resulted in the expansion and migration of Dominican gangs such as the Trinitarios.

Figure 5. Trinitarios Insignia

Source: ATF

This has led to an increase in drug trafficking, robberies, violent assaults in the Tri-state area.

Haitian Gangs

Haitian gangs, such as the Florida-based Zoe Pound, have proliferated in many states primarily along the East Coast in recent years according to NGIC reporting. According to NGIC reporting, Haitian gangs are present in Connecticut, Florida, Georgia, Indiana, Maryland, Massachusetts, New Jersey, New York, North Carolina, South Carolina, and Texas.

- The Zoe Pound gang, a street gang founded in Miami, Florida by Haitian immigrants in the United States, is involved in drug trafficking, robbery, and related violent crime. In February 2010, 22 suspected Zoe Pound members in Chicago, Illinois, were charged with possession of and conspiracy to traffic powder and crack cocaine from Illinois to Florida, according to FBI reporting.[10]

- The Haitian Boys Posse and Custer Street Gang are involved in a myriad of criminal activities including drug and weapons trafficking, robberies, shootings and homicides along the East Coast.

Jamaican Gangs

Traditional Jamaican gangs operating in the United States are generally unsophisticated and lack a significant hierarchical structure, unlike gangs in Jamaica. Many active Jamaican gangs operating in the United States maintain ties to larger criminal organizations and gangs in Jamaica, such as the Shower Posse or the Spangler Posse. Jamaican gang members in the United States engage in drug and weapons trafficking.

> NGIC reporting indicates that Jamaican gangs are most active in California, Maryland, Missouri, and New Jersey.

NON-TRADITIONAL GANGS

Hybrid Gangs

The expansion of hybrid gangs—non-traditional gangs with multiple affiliations—is a continued phenomenon in many jurisdictions nationwide. Because of their multiple affiliations, ethnicities, migratory nature, and nebulous structure, hybrid gangs are difficult to track, identify, and target as they are transient and continuously evolving. Furthermore, these multi-ethnic, mixed-gender gangs pose a unique challenge to law enforcement because they are adopting national symbols and gang members often crossover from gang to gang. Hybrid gangs are of particular concern to law enforcement because members often escalate their criminal activity in order to gain attention and respect.

Hybrid gangs, which are present in at least 25 states, are fluid in size and structure, yet tend to adopt similar characteristics of larger urban gangs, including their own identifiers, rules, and recruiting methods.[11] Like most street gangs, hybrid gang members commit a multitude of street and violent crime.[12] Law enforcement reporting suggests that hybrid gangs have evolved from neighborhood crews that formed to expand drug trafficking, or from an absence of or loyalty to nationally recognized gangs in their region.

- Law enforcement officials in many jurisdictions nationwide report an increase in juvenile gang membership and violent crime among hybrid and local gangs, according to 2010 NGIC reporting.

- NGIC reporting indicates that hybrid gangs are dominating nationally recognized gangs in some jurisdictions and merging with other gangs to expand their membership.

Juggalos

The Juggalos, a loosely-organized hybrid gang, are rapidly expanding into many US communities. Although recognized as a gang in only four states, many Juggalos subsets exhibit gang-like behavior and engage in criminal activity and violence. Law enforcement officials in at least 21 states have identified criminal Juggalo sub-sets, according to NGIC reporting.[d]

---

[d] Juggalos are traditionally fans of the musical group the Insane Clown Posse. Arizona, California, Pennsylvania, and Utah are the only US states that recognize Juggalos as a gang.

Hybrid and Almighty Latin King Nation (ALKN) Gang Members Arrested on Drug Charges

In November 2010, hybrid gang members in Pontiac, Michigan, known the "New World Order," were charged along with members of the ALKN for numerous drug offenses. Several guns, drugs, dozens of cell phones and $10,000 in cash were seized by FBI, DEA and local police departments. Many of the gang members arrested were juveniles and young adults.

Source: Online article "7 Members of 2 Gangs n Pontiac Face Drug charges" MyFoxdetroit.com; November 14, 2010

- NGIC reporting indicates that Juggalo gangs are expanding in New Mexico primarily because they are attracted to the tribal and cultural traditions of the Native Americans residing nearby.

Most crimes committed by Juggalos are sporadic, disorganized, individualistic, and often involve simple assault, personal drug use and possession, petty theft, and vandalism. However, open source reporting suggests that a small number of Juggalos are forming more organized subsets and engaging in more gang-like criminal activity, such as felony assaults, thefts, robberies, and drug sales. Social networking websites are a popular conveyance for Juggalo sub-culture to communicate and expand.

- In January 2011, a suspected Juggalo member shot and wounded a couple in King County, Washington, according to open source reporting.[13]

Juggalos

Although law enforcement officials in Arizona, California, Pennsylvania, Utah, and Washington report the most Juggalo gang-related criminal activity, Juggalos are present in Colorado, Delaware, Florida, Illinois, Iowa, Kansas, Massachusetts, Michigan, New Mexico, New Hampshire, North Carolina, Oklahoma, Oregon, Pennsylvania, Tennessee, Texas, and Virginia, according to NGIC reporting.

Figure 6. Juggalo member

Source: ATF

Juggalos' disorganization and lack of structure within their groups, coupled with their transient nature, makes it difficult to classify them and identify their members and migration patterns. Many criminal Juggalo subsets are comprised of transient or homeless individuals, according to law enforcement reporting. Most Juggalo criminal groups are not motivated to migrate based upon traditional needs of a gang. However, law enforcement reporting suggests that Juggalo criminal activity has increased over the past several years and has expanded to several other states. Transient, criminal Juggalo groups pose a threat to communities due to the potential for violence, drug use/sales, and their general destructive and violent nature.

- In January 2010, two suspected Juggalo associates were charged with beating and robbing an elderly homeless man.[14]

Gangs and Alien Smuggling, Human Trafficking, and Prostitution

Gang involvement in alien smuggling, human trafficking, and prostitution is increasing primarily due to their higher profitability and lower risks of detection and punishment than that of drug and weapons trafficking. Over the past year, federal, state, and local law enforcement officials in at least 35 states and US territories have reported that gangs in their jurisdictions are involved in alien smuggling, human trafficking, or prostitution.[e]

ALIEN SMUGGLING

Many street gangs are becoming involved in alien smuggling as a source of revenue. According to US law enforcement officials, tremendous incentive exists for gangs to diversify their criminal enterprises to include alien smuggling, which can be more lucrative and less risky than the illicit drug trade. Over the past two years numerous federal, state, and local law enforcement agencies nationwide have reported gang involvement in incidents of alien smuggling. In some instances, gang members were among those being smuggled across the border into the United States following deportation. In other cases, gang members facilitated the movement of migrants across the US-Mexico border.[f]

Increasing Coordination between Mexican Drug Cartels, Alien Smuggling Networks, and US Based Gangs

Federal, state, and local law enforcement officials are observing a growing nexus between the Mexican drug cartels, illegal alien smuggling rings, and US-based gangs. The alien smuggling networks that operate along the Southwest border are unable to move human cargo through drug cartel controlled corridors without paying a fee. The typical Mexican illegal alien now pays approximately $1,200 to $2,500 for entry into the United States. The fee is considerably higher for aliens smuggled from countries other than Mexico, which may even be more alluring for the cartels. It is estimated that criminals earn billions of dollars each year by smuggling aliens through Mexico into the United States.

Source: House Committee on Homeland Security, US Congress

Figure 7. An immigrant is smuggled in a vehicle

Source: FBI

---

[e] **Alien smuggling** involves facilitating the illegal entry of aliens for financial or other tangible benefits. It can involve an individual or a criminal organization. Business relationships typically cease once the individual has reached their destination. **Human trafficking** involves recruitment, transportation, and harboring of persons through force, fraud, or coercion for labor or services that result in slavery, involuntary servitude, or debt bondage. The business relationship does not end and often becomes exploitative and violent.

[f] According to the United Nations, over 90 percent of Mexican migrants illegally entering the United States are assisted by professional smugglers. Although most of the migrants are smuggled in trucks, many have been smuggled by rail, on foot, and tunnels.

The Barrio Azteca, Mexican Mafia, MS-13, 18th Street Gang, and Somali gangs have all reportedly been involved in alien smuggling, according to NGIC and law enforcement reporting.

- In October 2009, ICE agents in Los Angeles, California, arrested suspects linked to a drug trafficking and alien smuggling ring with close ties to the Drew Street clique of the Avenues (Sureño) street gang in Los Angeles. The ring allegedly smuggled more than 200 illegal aliens per year into the United States from Mexico, concealing them in trucks and hidden compartments of vehicles and then hiding them in a store house in Los Angeles (See Figure 8).[15]

HUMAN TRAFFICKING

Human trafficking is another source of revenue for some gangs. Victims—typically women and children— are often forced, coerced, or led with fraudulent pretense into prostitution and forced labor.[16] The Bloods, MS-13, Sureños, and Somali gangs have been reportedly involved in human trafficking, according to multiple law enforcement and NGIC reporting.

- Some gangs in the New England area are combining human trafficking and drug trafficking operations, where females are used to courier drugs and participate in prostitution.

- In November 2010, federal law enforcement officials indicted 29 members of a Somalian gang in Minneapolis for operating an interstate sex trafficking ring that sold and transported underage African-American and Somalian females from Minneapolis, Minnesota, to Columbus, Ohio, and Nashville, Tennessee, for prostitution, according to FBI and ICE reporting.[17]

PROSTITUTION

Prostitution is also a major source of income for many gangs. Gang members often operate as pimps, luring or forcing at-risk, young females into prostitution and controlling them through violence and psychological abuse.[9] Asian gangs, Bloods, Crips, Gangster Disciples, MS-13, Sureños, Vice Lords, and members of OMGs are involved in prostitution operations, according to FBI, NGIC, and multiple law enforcement reporting.

---

[9] For years, gang members used Internet websites to advertise the sale of their victims. However, recently several Internet sites including Craigslist have eliminated their erotic services personal advertisement sections.

NGIC law enforcement partners report that gangs in their jurisdiction are involved in prostitution, some of which involves child prostitution.

- Prostitution is reportedly the second largest source of income for San Diego, California, gangs. According to November 2010 open source reporting, African-American street gangs in San Diego are pimping young females to solicit males.[18]

Gangs and Criminal Organizations

GANGS & DRUG TRAFFICKING ORGANIZATIONS

Many US-based gangs have established strong working relationships with Central America and Mexico-based DTOs to perpetuate the smuggling of drugs across the US-Mexico and US-Canada borders. MDTOs control most of the cocaine, heroin, methamphetamine, and marijuana trafficked into the United States from Mexico and regularly employ lethal force to protect their drug shipments in Mexico and while crossing the US-Mexico border, according to NGIC and NDIC reporting.[h]

Mexican Drug Trafficking Organizations

MDTOs are among the most prominent DTOs largely because of their control over the production of most drugs consumed in the United States. They are known to regularly collaborate with US-based street and prison gang members and occasionally work with select OMG and White Supremacist groups, purely for financial gain (see Appendix B). The prospect of financial gain is resulting in the suspension of traditional racial and ideological

Many Los Angeles-based Sinaloa cartel members use local gang members to assist in or commit kidnappings, acquire or sell drugs, and collect drug proceeds.

Source: DHS September 2010; DEA November 2010

division among US prison gangs, providing MDTOs the means to further expand their influence over drug trafficking in the United States.[19] NDIC reporting indicates that Hispanic and African American street gangs are expanding their influence over drug distribution in rural and suburban areas and acquire drugs directly from MDTOs in Mexico or along the Southwest border.[20]

NGIC law enforcement partners report that gangs in their jurisdiction have ties to Mexican criminal organizations, such as MDTOs.

- Well-established US prison gangs such as the Hermanos de Pistoleros Latinos (HPL), La Eme, the Texas Syndicate, Barrio Azteca and the Tango Blast are reportedly aligned with or connected to MDTOs.

- NDIC reporting indicates that street gangs such as the Latin Kings, MS-13, Sureños, and Norteños maintain working relationships with MDTOs.[21] Sureños in California and South Carolina maintain an association with the Los Zetas Cartel in Mexico, according to 2010 NGIC reporting.

---

[h] MDTOs control up to 80 percent of wholesale cocaine distribution in the United States.

US-based Gangs with Ties to MDTOs

Arizona New Mexican Mafia	Mara Salvatrucha (MS-13)
Aryan Brotherhood	Mexican Mafia
Avenues	Mongols
Bandidos	Norteños
Barrio Azteca	Satins Disciples
Barrio Westside	Sureños
Black Guerilla Family	Tango Blast
Bloods	Texas Mexican Mafia (Mexikanemi)
California Mexican Mafia (Eme)	Texas Syndicate
Crips	Tri-City Bombers
Hardtimes 13	Vagos
Happytown Pomona	Vatos Locos
Hells Angels	Westside Nogalitas
Hermanos de Pistoleros Latinos (HPL)	Wetback Power
	Wonder Boys
La Nuestra Familia	18th Street Gang
Latin Kings	
Lennox 13	

Figure 8. Mexican Drug Cartels

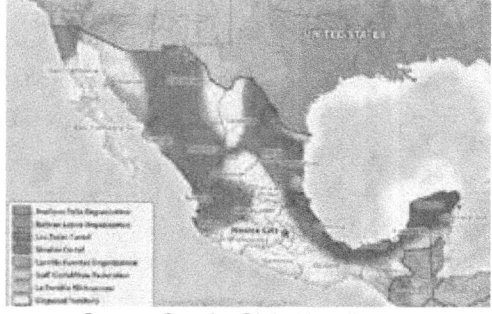

Source: Stratfor Global Intelligence

• According to 2010 California Department of Corrections and Rehabilitation (CDCR) and open source reporting, some Aryan Brotherhood and La Eme prison gang members—bitter rivals inside prison—work together with MDTOs to smuggle drugs into California and prisons, steal vehicles, smuggle illegal weapons into Mexico, and intimidate rivals of the Mexican cartels.[22]

MDTOs contract with street and prison gangs along the Southwest border to enforce and secure smuggling operations in Mexico and the United States, particularly in California and Texas border communities.[23] Gang members who are US citizens are valuable to MDTOs, as they can generally cross the US-Mexico border with less law enforcement scrutiny and are therefore less likely to have illicit drug loads interdicted.[24] MDTOs use street and prison gang members in Mexico, Texas, and California to protect smuggling routes, collect debts, transport illicit goods, including drugs and weapons, and execute rival traffickers.[25] Many of these crimes are committed in exchange for money and drugs, and as a result, street and prison gangs in the United States have gained greater control over drug distribution in rural and suburban areas. Gang members, including Barrio Azteca, MS-13 and Sureños have been intercepted driving with weapons and currency toward Mexico from such states as California, Colorado, Georgia, and Texas according to open source reporting.

Gangs' increased collaboration with MDTOs has altered the dynamics of the drug trade at the wholesale level. US gangs, which traditionally served as the primary organized retail or mid-level distributor of drugs in most major US cities, are now purchasing drugs directly from the cartels, thereby eliminating the mid-level wholesale dealer. Furthermore, advanced technology, such as

Major Mexican Drug Trafficking Organizations

Arellano Felix	Los Zetas
Beltran Leyva	Sinaloa
Vicente Carrillo-Fuentes	La Familia Michoacana
Gulf Cartel	

wireless Internet and Voice over Internet Protocol (VoIP) capabilities, has made the recruitment, collaboration, and coordination of criminal activity more efficient and lucrative, and allows direct contact between the gangs and DTOs.[26] To increase their control over drug trafficking in smaller markets, street gangs have acquired large wholesale quantities of drugs at lower prices directly from DTOs in Mexico and along the US Southwest border.[27]

- Recent intelligence indicates that the MDTO La Familia Michoacana has established US-based command-and-control groups which report to leaders in Mexico who manage street-level distribution in US cities.[28]

GANGS AND ORGANIZED CRIMINAL GROUPS
January 2010 FBI reporting indicates that some OMGs and street gangs are closely collaborating with African, Asian, Eurasian, and Italian organized criminal groups to facilitate street-level crimes such as extortion, enforcement, debt collection, and money laundering.

- In May 2010, New Jersey authorities indicted 34 members of the Lucchese crime family on racketeering, weapons offenses, bribery, money laundering, and conspiracy charges. The investigation revealed that members of the Lucchese family in New Jersey were working with the Nine

Trey Gangster Bloods to smuggle drugs and cell phones into the East Jersey State Prison for fellow inmates, according to open source reporting.[29]

NGIC reporting indicates that some gangs are suspected of associating with African, Asian, and Eurasian criminal groups in California and Washington.[i]

- Law enforcement officials in Washington suspect that some Asian gangs, including the Oriental Boyz and the Tiny Rascal Gangsters, are involved with Asian organized crime and marijuana cultivating groups.

- In February 2011, authorities in southern California charged 99 Armenian Power gang members with kidnapping, extortion, bank fraud, and drug trafficking. Armenian Power members reportedly have ties to high-level crime figures in Armenia, Russia, and Georgia.[30]

---

[i] Eurasian criminal groups include Albanian, Armenian, Eastern European, and Russian criminal enterprises.

Chart 3. Gang Associations with Criminal Organizations.

The NGIC collected intelligence from law enforcement officials nationwide in an effort to identify associations between gangs and criminal organizations. The following figures represent the percentage of law enforcement who report that gangs in their jurisdiction have ties to various criminal organizations.

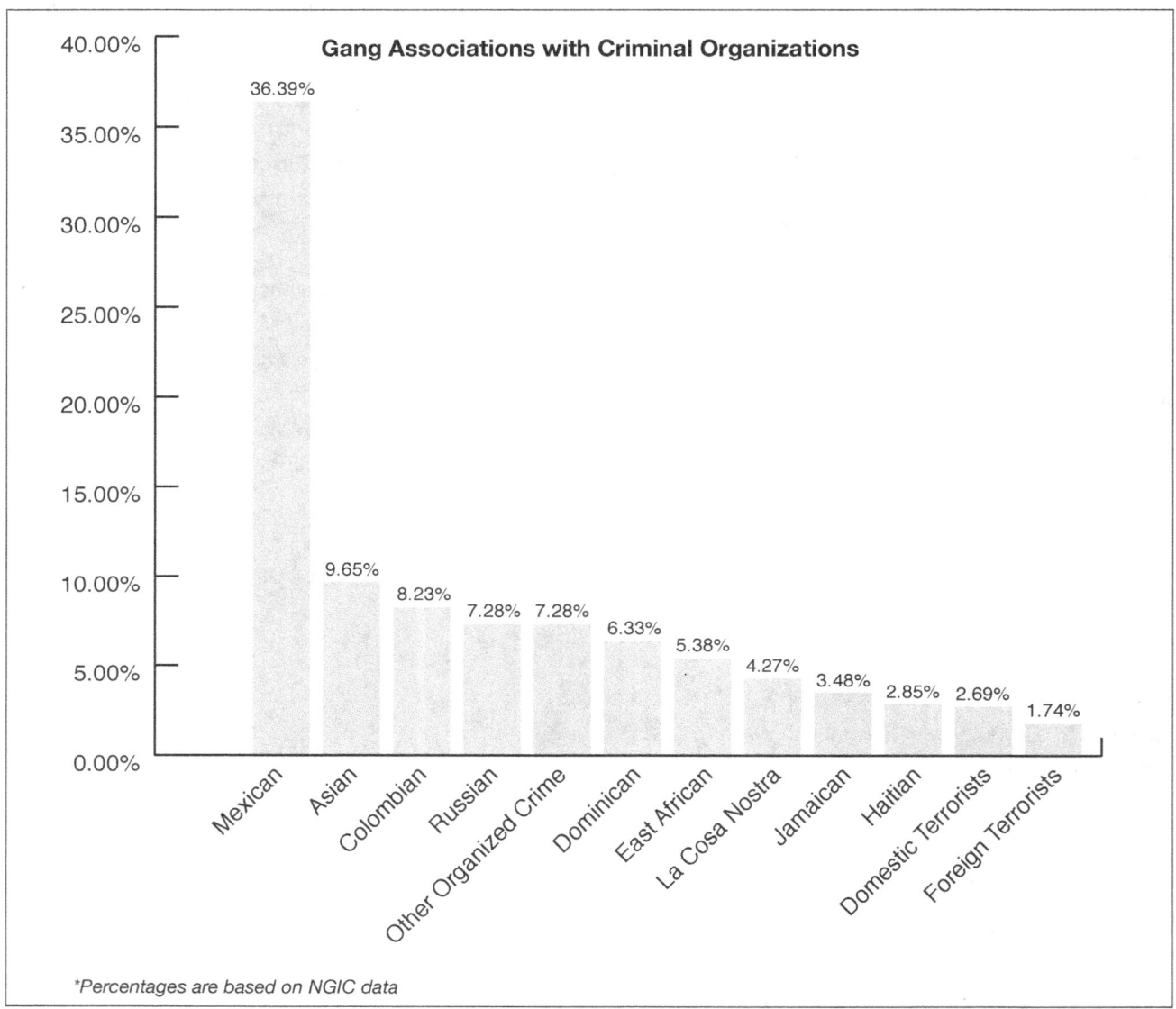

Figure 9. A US prison yard

Figure 10. Incarcerated MS-13 Members

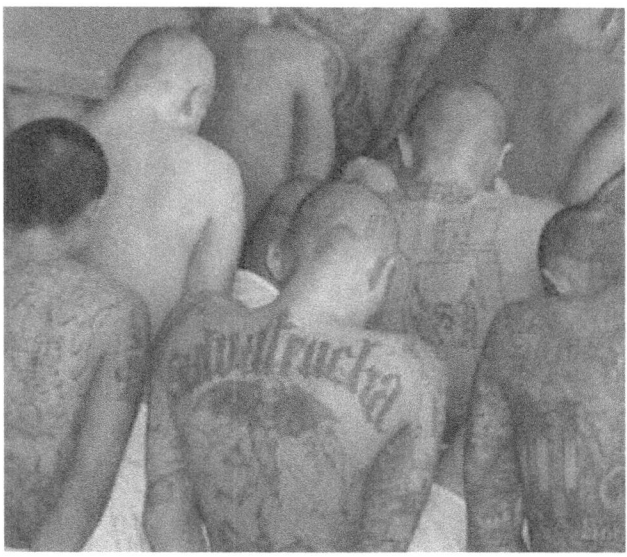

Gangs and Corrections Issues

Prison gang-related crime and violence in the nation's corrections system poses a significant threat to facility employees and a growing threat in many communities. Once incarcerated, most street gang members join an established prison gang to ensure their protection. Based on data provided by federal and state correctional agencies, the NGIC estimates that there are approximately 231,136 gang members incarcerated in federal and state prisons nationwide. Their large numbers and dominant presence allows prison gangs to employ bribery, intimidation, and violence to exert influence and control over many correctional facilities. Violent disputes over control of drug territory and enforcement of drug debts frequently occur among incarcerated gang members.

PRISON/STREET GANG CONNECTIONS

Many incarcerated gang members continue to engage in gang activities following incarceration and use their connections inside prison to commit crime in the community. Prison gang members influence and control gang activity on the street, and exploit street gangs for money and other resources.

> Law enforcement officials report associations between street gang members and incarcerated gang members in their area.

- MS-13 members send funds not only to gang members on the street and in prison, but also to gang members in El Salvador, according to NGIC reporting.

PRISON/FAMILY CONNECTION

A gang member's incarceration often prompts his or her family to move closer to the correctional facility where the gang member is being housed. In some cases, family members assist or facilitate gang criminal activity and recruiting.

Family members of gangs operate as outside facilitators, serving as messengers, drug couriers, or in any capacity benefiting the gang. Outside facilitators are provided instructions by the incarcerated gang member, often during a social or legal visit, and in turn pass this information to gang members on the streets. Family members have also been used to assist prison escapes and smuggle contraband into correctional facilities, allowing incarcerated gang members to continue their operations inside prison.

Gangs in contact with incarcerated gang members

18th Street	La Nuestra Familia
415 Kumi	Latin Kings
Arizona New Mexican Mafia	Los Carnales
	MS-13
Aryan Brotherhood	Nazi Low Riders
Aryan Brotherhood of Texas	Ñetas
Aryan Circle	Norteños
Bandidos	Northern Riders
Barrio Azteca	Northern Structure
Black Guerilla Family	Outlaws
Black Gangster Disciples	Paisas
	Raza Unida
Black P-Stone Nation	Simon City Royals
Bloods	Skinheads
California Mexican Mafia	Sureños
	Syndicato De Nuevo Mexico
Colorado Aryan Brotherhood	Texas Chicano Brotherhood
Crips	Texas Mexican Mafia (Mexikanemi-EMI)
Dead Man Inc.	
Dirty White Boys	Texas Syndicate
Gangster Disciples (GD)	United Blood Nation
Grupo 25 (G-25)	Valluco Tango Blast
Grupo 27 (G-27)	Vice Lords
Hells Angels (MC)	West Texas Tangos
Hermanos de Pistoleros Latinos (HPL)	

COMMUNICATION

Incarcerated gang members often rely on family, friends, corrupt lawyers and corrections personnel to transmit their messages to gang members on the street. Incarcerated gang members exploit attorney-client privileges, which include unmonitored visiting and legal mail, to pass coded or concealed communications.[j]

Contraband Cell Phones

Smuggled cell phones are a continuing problem for prison administrators in correctional facilities throughout the country. Smuggled cell phones and Smart Phones afford incarcerated gang members more influence and control over street gangs through unrestricted access and unmonitored conversations via voice calling, Internet access, text messaging, email, and social networking websites. Instances of violence directed by inmates using mobile devices are also a growing concern for corrections officials. Incarcerated gang members communicate covertly with illegal cell phones to plan or direct criminal activities such as drug distribution, assault, and murder.

> Cell phones smuggled into correctional facilities pose the greatest threat to institution safety, according to NGIC and BOP reporting.

- In 2010 a New Jersey inmate was prosecuted for using a contraband cell phone to order the murder of his former girlfriend in retaliation for her cooperation with police regarding an investigation involving the inmate.[31]

---

[j] Legal mail refers to any correspondence sent to or received from a legal professional. Gang members may disguise their correspondence to resemble legal mail so that it is exempt from inspection.

Illegal Cell Phones in California Prisons

The majority of illegal cell phones in California prisons are smuggled in by visitors or correctional staff. Many cell phones have also been discovered in legal mail and quarterly packages. In 2010, more than 10,000 illegal cell phones were confiscated from prisoners in California.

Historically, correctional staff who have been caught smuggling phones have been successfully prosecuted only when the phone was connected to a more serious charge such as drug distribution, and district attorney offices rarely prosecute unless a more serious offense is involved. In March 2011, legislation was approved in the California State Senate to criminalize the use of cell phones in prison, including penalties for both smugglers and inmates.

Sources: US Bureau of Prisons and CDCR; California State Senate Press Release, 22 March 2011

- In March 2010, an off-duty captain in the South Carolina Department of Corrections was shot in his home by an armed intruder. Although the captain survived, the assault had been ordered by a South Carolina inmate using a smuggled cell phone.[32]

LEADERSHIP

Gang members who have been incarcerated are often more respected on the streets by younger gang members, which makes it easier to establish or re-establish themselves in leadership positions and order younger gang members to commit crimes.[k] These gang leaders also use connections made in prison to establish contacts and criminal networks in the community, which allows them to more successfully control gang operations. Also, in the wake of leadership disorganization at the street level due to indictments and arrests, a released gang member may find it easy to use his influence and status as an 'original gangster' (OG) or Veterano to assume control of the gang.

> **Law enforcement officials report that released prison gang members in some jurisdictions are establishing or re-establishing leadership roles or active roles in local gangs.**

PRISON RADICALIZATION

Gang members' vulnerability to radicalization and recruitment for involvement in international or domestic terrorism organizations is a growing concern to law enforcement. Gang members' perceptions of disenfranchisement from or rejection of mainstream society and resentment towards authority makes them more susceptible to joining such groups and can be attractive and easy targets for radicalization by extremist groups.

> **NGIC reporting indicates that incarcerated gang members in some jurisdictions are adopting radical religious views in prison.**

---

[k] Gang members leave prison with the knowledge and connections that allow them to identify with a national gang which will garner them greater respect and "street credibility" within their community.

Prison gangs that tend to be dedicated to political or social issues are often more susceptible to influence by extremist ideologies. In some instances, prison gang members may even emulate various terrorist movements by embracing their symbolism and ideology to enhance the gang's own militant image within the prison setting.

Prison and street gang members are also susceptible on an individual basis to radicalization. Various correctional agencies have reported individual members of the Black Peace Stones, Crips, Latin Kings, and Insane Latin Disciples embracing radical ideologies.

Gang Infiltration of Corrections, Law Enforcement, and Government

Gang infiltration of law enforcement, government, and correctional agencies poses a significant security threat due to the access criminals have to sensitive information pertaining to investigations or protected persons. Gang members serving in law enforcement agencies and correctional facilities may compromise security and criminal investigations and operations, while acquiring knowledge and training in police tactics and weapons. Corrupt law enforcement officers and correctional staff have assisted gang members in committing crimes and have impeded investigations.

> NGIC reporting indicates that gang members in at least 57 jurisdictions, including California, Florida, Tennessee, and Virginia, have applied for or gained employment within judicial, police, or correctional agencies.

- A Crip gang member applied for a law enforcement position in Oklahoma.

- OMGs engage in routine and systematic exploitation and infiltration of law enforcement and government infrastructures to protect and perpetrate their criminal activities. OMGs regularly solicit information of intelligence value from government or law enforcement employees.

NGIC reporting indicates that gang members in at least 72 jurisdictions have compromised or corrupted judicial, law enforcement, or correctional staff within the past three years.

- In November 2010, a parole worker in New York was suspended for relaying confidential information to a Bloods gang member in Albany, according to open source reporting.[33]

- In July 2010, a Riverside County, California detention center sheriff deputy was convicted of assisting her incarcerated Eme boyfriend with murdering two witnesses in her boyfriend's case.[34]

- In April 2010, a former Berwyn, Illinois police officer pleaded guilty to charges of conspiracy to commit racketeering and to obstruct justice for his part in assisting an OMG member in targeting and burglarizing rival businesses.[35]

Gangs and Indian Country

Native American gang presence has increased on Indian Reservations and in federal and state prison systems throughout the United States over the past few years, according to Bureau of Justice Statistics reporting.[36l] Native American gang members, operating on numerous reservations throughout the United States, are emulating Hispanic gangs such as the Barrio Aztecas, Norteños, and Sureños; African American gangs such as the Bloods and Crips; and predominately Caucasian gangs such as the Juggalos. Some gangs, such as the Native Mob and Native Pride—which primarily operates in North Dakota, Minnesota, South Dakota, and Wisconsin—formed in the prison system and then expanded to reservations, according to NGIC reporting. Although most gangs in Indian Country are disorganized, lack significant structure and ties to national-level gangs, and are incapable of attaining control over large geographic areas or populations, some are involved in serious crimes and violent activities and utilize Indian Reservations to facilitate and expand their drug operations.

The growth of gangs on Indian Reservations is heavily influenced by the urban gang culture and media attention. Gang members on Indian Reservations often emulate national-level gangs and adopt names and identifiers from nationally recognized urban gangs. However, emulation is most often limited to identifiers—colors, signs, symbols, names—and leadership structure is often loosely organized or absent. NGIC reporting indicates that national-level gangs such as the Barrio Azteca, Bloods, Crips, Mexican Mafia, and Norteños are operating on a number of Indian Reservations. Native American gang members on reservations are also

---

l According to the Bureau of Justice Statistics, the number of Native Americans incarcerated in jails and prisons nationwide increased by approximately 2.5 percent from 2007 to 2008.

Indian Country and the US Border

The shared international border and geography of some Indian Reservations make it conducive to cross-border drug trafficking activity while also inhibiting interdiction efforts. Increased security at US/Mexican borders has resulted in the discovery of illicit marijuana farms from California to South Dakota, primarily operated by Mexican gangs. Tighter border security makes it difficult for MDTOs to smuggle marijuana north thus raising the price of marijuana in the United States higher than in Mexico. Marijuana (stems and leaves) grown in Mexico costs $500 to $700 per pound, whereas a pound of marijuana grown in Washington State can cost $2,500 to $6,000 when sold on the East Coast.

Online News Article; The Wall Street Journal; "Mexican Pot Gangs Infiltrate Indian Reservations in US;" 5 November 2009; available at http://online.wsj.com/article/ SB125736987377028727.html.

involved in gang-related activity with gang members in communities outside of reservations.

NGIC reporting indicates that urban gangs such as the Norteños and Sureños associate and/ or influence the gang culture on several Indian Reservations.

In some jurisdictions, Native American gang members are associated with or involved in gang-related criminal activity with gang members off the reservation, including drug distribution, money laundering, assaults, and intimidation. Partnerships are often established for financial gain, drug distribution, and to evade law enforcement.

Figure 12. Graffiti on Ft. Apache-San Carlos Indian Reservation

Source: FBI

- The Warm Springs Indian Reservation in Oregon is becoming an ideal location for illicit marijuana farms because of its fertile grounds and isolated location. Within the past few years authorities have seized at least 12,000 harvested adult marijuana plants with an estimated street value of $10 million.[37]

Geography, as well as the extent of law enforcement monitoring of the reservations, make some Indian Reservations conducive to cross-border drug trafficking.

- As much as 20 percent of all high-potency marijuana produced in Canada each year is smuggled through the St. Regis Mohawk Reservation in New York, according to NDIC reporting.

- Marijuana produced in Mexico is transported by MDTOs through the Tohono O'odham Reservation in Arizona largely due to the 75 miles of lightly patrolled border with Mexico, according to NDIC reporting.

Gangs and the Military

Gang recruitment of active duty military personnel constitutes a significant criminal threat to the US military. Members of nearly every major street gang, as well as some prison gangs and OMGs, have been reported on both domestic and international military installations, according to NGIC analysis and multiple law enforcement reporting. Through transfers and deployments, military-affiliated gang members expand their culture and operations to new regions nationwide and worldwide, undermining security and law enforcement efforts to combat crime. Gang members with military training pose a unique threat to law enforcement personnel because of their distinctive weapons and combat training skills and their ability to transfer these skills to fellow gang members.

NGIC reporting indicates that law enforcement officials in at least 100 jurisdictions have come into contact with, detained, or arrested an active duty or former military gang member within the past three years.

- Gang members have been reported in every branch of the US military[m], although a large proportion of these gang members and dependent gang members of military personnel are affiliated with the US Army, Army Reserves, and National Guard branches.

Many street gang members join the military to escape the gang lifestyle or as an alternative to incarceration, but often revert back to their gang associations once they encounter other gang members in the military. Other gangs target the US military and defense systems

_____

[m] US military branches include Army, Air Force, Coast Guard, Marines, Navy, Army Reserves, and National Guard.

Figure 13. 'Support your local Hells Angels' graffiti on military vehicle in Iraq

Source: FBI

Figure 14. A soldier in a combat zone throwing gang signs

Source: FBI

As of April 2011, the NGIC has identified members of at least 53 gangs whose members have served in or are affiliated with US military. Among the identified gangs with military-trained members are street gangs such as the Asian Boyz, Bloods, Crips, Gangster Disciples, Latin Kings, MS-13, Sureños, Tiny Rascal Gangsters, and the Juggalos; the Aryan Brotherhood, Barrio Azteca, and Texas Syndicate prison gangs; and OMGs including the Bandidos, Hells Angels, Mongols, Outlaws, and Vagos. Some gangs, particularly OMGs, actively recruit members with military training or advise members without criminal records to join the military for necessary weapons and combat training.

- Younger gang members without criminal records are attempting to join the military, as well as concealing tattoos and gang affiliation during the recruitment process, according to NGIC reporting.

Deployments have resulted in integrating gang members with service members and/or dependents on or near overseas military installations, including those in Afghanistan, Germany, Iraq, Italy, Japan, and South Korea. US military officials have reported a rise in gang graffiti both on and off post in Afghanistan and Iraq (see Figure 14).

to expand their territory, facilitate criminal activity such as weapons and drug trafficking, or to receive weapons and combat training that they may transfer back to their gang. Incidents of weapons theft and trafficking may have a negative impact on public safety or pose a threat to law enforcement officials.

Table 3. Gangs with Members Who have Served in the US Military

GANG NAME	TYPE	MILITARY BRANCH(S)
18th Street Gang	Street	Army, Marines, Navy
Aryan Brotherhood	Prison	Army, Marines, Navy
Asian Boyz	Street	Army
Asian Crips	Street	Army
Avenues Gang	Street	Marines
Bandidos	OMG	Army, Marines
Barrio Azteca	Prison	Marines
Black Disciples	Street	Army, Marines, Navy
Black Guerilla Family*	Prison	Army
Bloods	Street	Army, Army Reserves, Coast Guard, Marines, Navy
Brotherhood	OMG	Marines
Crips	Street	Army, Air Force, Marines, Navy
Devils Disciples	OMG	Unknown
East Side Longos	Street	Army, Special Forces
Florencia 13	Street	Army, Marines
Fresno Bulldogs	Street	National Guard, Marines
Gangster Disciples	Street	Army, Marines, Navy, National Guard
Georgia Boys (Folk Nation)	Street	Army
Haitian Mob	Street	Army
Hells Angels	OMG	All branches
Iron Horsemen	OMG	Army
Juggalos/ICP	Street	Army, Air Force
Korean Dragon Family	Street	Marines
Latin Kings	Street	Army, Army Reserves, Marines, Navy
Legion of Doom	OMG	Air Force

GANG NAME	TYPE	MILITARY BRANCH(S)
Life is War	Street	Army
Los Zetas	Street	Army
Maniac Latin Disciples	Street	Marines
Mexican Posse 13	Street	Army
Military Misfits	OMG	Marines, Navy
Molochs	OMG	Marines
Mongols	OMG	Marines, Navy
Moorish Nation	Separatist	Army
MS-13	Street	Army, Marines, Navy
Norteños	Street	Army, Marines, National Guard, Navy
Outlaws	OMG	All branches
Peckerwoods	Street	Marines, Navy, National Guard, Reserves
Red Devils	OMG	Army/ Coast Guard
Simon City Royals	Street	Navy
Sons of Hell	OMG	Marines
Sons of Samoa	Street	Army
Southside Locos	Street	Army
Sureños	Street	Army, Marines, Navy
Tango Blast	Prison	Army*
Texas Syndicate	Prison	Army, Marines
Tiny Rascal Gangsters	Street	Army
United Blood Nation	Street	Army
Vagos	OMG	Army, Marines, Navy
Vatos Locos	Street	Army
Vice Lords	Street	Army
Wah Ching Gang	Street	Army
Warlocks	OMG	Air Force, Marines

* Only gang graffiti was identified

Figure 15. The Southwest Border Region

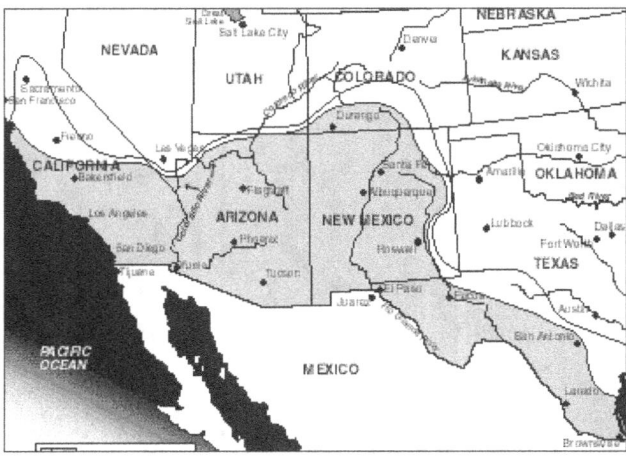

Source: America.gov

Gangs and the US Border

THE SOUTHWEST BORDER

The US Southwest Border region[n] represents a continuing criminal threat to the United States. The rugged, rural, and porous area along the nearly 2,000 miles of contiguous US-Mexican territory invites widespread criminal activity, including drug and arms trafficking, alien smuggling, human trafficking, extortion, kidnapping, and public corruption. US-based gangs, MDTOs, and other criminal enterprises in both the United States and Mexico are readily exploiting this fluid region and incur enormous profit by establishing wide-reaching drug networks; assisting in the smuggling drugs, arms, and illegal immigrants; and serving as enforcers for MDTO interests on the US side of the border.

Violence in Mexico—particularly in its northern border states—has escalated with over 34,000 murders committed in Mexico over the past four years.[38] While intensified scrutiny from Mexican law enforcement has forced significant disruptions in several dangerous MDTOs, such disruptions have also served to disrupt the balance of power among these organizations. This has prompted drug cartel rivalries to employ more aggressive tactics as they attempt to assert control over the Southwest border region and its highly lucrative drug trafficking corridors.[39] Although the majority of the violence from feuding drug cartels occurs in Mexico,[o] Mexican drug cartel activity has fueled crime in the porous US Southwest Border region, where easy access to weapons, a high demand for drugs, ample opportunity for law enforcement corruption, and a large Hispanic population ripe for recruitment and exploitation exists.[40]

Hispanic prison gangs along the Southwest border region are strengthening their ties with MDTOs to acquire wholesale quantities of drugs, according to NDIC reporting.[41] In exchange for a consistent drug supply, US-based gangs smuggle and distribute drugs, collect drug proceeds, launder money, smuggle weapons, commit kidnappings, and serve as lookouts and enforcers on behalf of the MDTOs. MDTOs subsequently profit from increased drug circulation in the United States, while US-based gangs have access to a consistent drug supply which expands their influence, power, and ability to recruit.[42]

---

[n] The US Southwest Border includes the southern borders of California, Arizona, New Mexico, and Texas.

[o] Although some US and local law enforcement officials maintain that violent crime in Southwest Border states has decreased in the past few years, the effects of such violence, including drug trafficking activity and migration patterns of Mexican citizens fleeing the violence in Northern Mexico, are most acutely reflected in the US Southwest Border Region. Furthermore, as the point of entry for the vast majority of illicit drugs that are smuggled into the United States, the Southwest Border Region is most susceptible to any spillover violence.

According to NDIC reporting, more than 45 percent of law enforcement agencies in the Southwestern United States report that gangs in their jurisdiction are moderately to highly involved in drug activity, while 30 percent indicate that street gang involvement in drug activity increased within the past year.

Gang-related activity and violence has increased along the Southwest border region, as US-based gangs seek to prove their worth to the drug cartels, compete with other gangs for favor, and act as US-based enforcers for cartels which involves home invasions, robbery, kidnapping, and murder.

- In July 2010, Mexican authorities arrested two members of the Barrio Azteca for the murders of a US Consulate employee and her husband in Juarez, Mexico. The gang, who allegedly committed the murders on behalf of the Juarez Cartel, has also made several threats against law enforcement officials.[43p]

Arrangements between gangs operating along the Southwest border and MDTOs are the result of physical proximity and strong familial ties that many US-based Hispanic gang members retain with family and friends in Mexico.

NORTHERN BORDER

Gangs pose a growing problem for law enforcement along the US-Canada border, particularly the border areas in the New England and Pacific Regions. Gangs smuggle drugs, cigarettes, firearms, and immigrants across the US-Canada borders, according to NDIC reporting.[44] Members of several regional- and national-level

---

[p] The Barrio Azteca works for the Juarez Cartel on both the US and Mexican sides of the border.

Los Zetas Drug Trafficking Organization

Los Zetas organization was established in the late 1990s as the enforcement arm of the Gulf Cartel drug trafficking organization to protect and expand the Gulf Cartel's operations. Consisting of highly trained soldiers who defected from the Mexican Special Air Mobile Force Group (GAFE), the Zetas have evolved from a wing of the Gulf Cartel into their own drug trafficking organization.

Figure 16. Los Zetas Commando Medallion

Source: ATF

gangs, including Asian Boyz, Hells Angels, and Outlaws, smuggle large quantities of illicit drugs across the US-Canada border in New England, often conducting their smuggling operations in association with members of transnational criminal and drug trafficking organizations. According to law enforcement officials in the Pacific Region, members of several gangs, including the Hells Angels and Asian gangs, engage in cross-border criminal activity in their jurisdictions.

- Hells Angels members have reportedly smuggled MDMA (Ecstasy) from British Columbia, Canada into Bellingham, Washington, according to 2010 open source reporting.

- Asian DTOs smuggle large quantities of MDMA through and between ports of entry along the US–Canada border, according to 2010 NDIC reporting.[45]

Canadian DTOs smuggle significant amounts of cash generated from the US distribution of Canada-produced drugs into Canada, according to NDIC reporting. The Akwesasne Territory, which straddles the US–Canada border, is one of the most prominent smuggling corridors for Canada-bound bulk cash. The topography of the US-Canada border is conducive to bulk cash smuggling because currency interdiction by law enforcement officials is often hampered by the border's length and rugged terrain.[46]

Gangs, Technology, and Communication

Gangs are becoming increasingly savvy and are embracing new and advanced technology to facilitate criminal activity and enhance their criminal operations. Prepaid cell phones, social networking and microblogging websites, VoIP systems, virtual worlds, and gaming systems enable gang members to communicate globally and discreetly. Gangs are also increasingly employing advanced countermeasures to monitor and target law enforcement while engaging in a host of criminal activity.

Gang members routinely utilize the Internet to communicate with one another, recruit, promote their gang, intimidate rivals and police, conduct gang business, showcase illegal exploits, and facilitate criminal activity such as drug trafficking, extortion, identity theft, money laundering, and prostitution. Social networking, microblogging, and video-sharing websites—such as Facebook, YouTube, and Twitter—are now more accessible,

Internet Use for Propaganda, Intimidation, and Recruitment

According to open sources and law enforcement reporting, since 2005, MDTOs have exploited blogs and popular websites like YouTube and MySpace for propaganda and intimidation. MDTOs have posted hundreds of videos depicting interrogations or executions of rival MDTO members. Other postings include video montages of luxury vehicles, weapons, and money set to the music of songs with lyrics that glorify the drug lifestyle. While some of these postings may offer specific recruitment information, they serve more as tools for propaganda and intimidation.

versatile, and allow tens of thousands of gang members to easily communicate, recruit, and form new gang alliances nationwide and worldwide.[q]

NGIC reporting indicates that a majority of gang members use the Internet for recruitment, gang promotion, and cyber-bullying or intimidation. Many also use the Internet for identity theft, computer hacking, and phishing schemes.

---

[q] These estimates were derived from the large number of gang members populating social networking Web sites such as the Hoodup.com, Facebook, and MySpace.

- According to NGIC reporting, gang recruitment and intimidation is heavily facilitated through the Internet. Gangs use social networking sites such as Facebook to promote their gang, post photos of their gang lifestyle, and display their bravado, which ultimately influences other youth to join gangs.

- NGIC law enforcement partners report that gangs in their jurisdiction are frequently using the Internet to recruit and communicate with gang members throughout the region, nationwide, and in Central and South America. Law enforcement officials in Texas report that incarcerated gang members use Facebook and MySpace to recruit.

- Police in Missouri report a rise in "promotion teams"—often consisting of gang members—using Internet chat rooms to promote clubs and parties for a fee, according to NGIC reporting.

The proliferation of social networking websites has made gang activity more prevalent and lethal – moving gangs from the streets into cyber space. Gang members, criminals, and drug traffickers are using the Internet not only to recruit and build their social networks, but to expand and operate their criminal networks without the proximity once needed for communication. Likewise, youth in other regions and countries are influenced by what they see online and may be encouraged to connect with or emulate a gang, facilitating the global spread of gang culture.

- Gang members in Missouri and Nebraska are increasingly using social media to recruit and communicate with other gang members, according to NGIC reporting.

Second Life Virtual World

Second Life is a computer-based virtual world with a simulated environment where users inhabit and interact via avatars, or graphical representations. The virtual world may depict a real world or a fantasy world. Users communicate through text-chat and real-time voice-based chat. Second Life provides versatility and anonymity and allows for covert communications. Because of its anonymity and versatility, gang members could potentially use Second Life to recruit, spread propaganda, commit other crimes such as drug trafficking, and receive training for real-world criminal operations.

Source: Information available at www.secondlife.com

According to information obtained from multiple state and federal law enforcement sources, incarcerated gang members are accessing micro-blogging and social networking web sites such as MocoSpace and Twitter with smuggled prepaid cellular telephones and using the messaging features to coordinate criminal activity.

Street gang members are also involved in cyber attacks, computer hacking, and phishing operations, often to commit identity theft and fraud.

Gangs and Weapons

Gang members are acquiring high-powered, military-style weapons and equipment, resulting in potentially lethal encounters with law enforcement officers, rival gang members, and innocent bystanders. Law enforcement officials in several regions nationwide report gang members in their jurisdiction are armed with military-style weapons, such as high-caliber semiautomatic rifles, semiautomatic variants of AK-47 assault rifles, grenades, and body armor.

Law enforcement officials in 34 jurisdictions report that the majority of gang-related crime is committed with firearms.

Gang members acquire firearms through a variety of means, including illegal purchases; straw purchases through surrogates or middle-men; thefts from individuals, vehicles, residences and commercial establishments; theft from law enforcement and military officials, from gang members with connections to military sources of supply, and from other gangs, according to multiple law enforcement and NGIC reporting.

Gang members are becoming more sophisticated and methodical in their methods of acquiring and purchasing firearms. Gang members often acquire their firearms through theft or through a middleman, often making a weapons trace more difficult.

Enlisted military personnel are also being utilized by gang members as a ready source for weapons.

- In November 2010, three former US Marines were arrested in Los Angeles, California, for selling illegal assault weapons to Florencia 13 gang members, according to open souce reporting.[47]

Figure 17. Weapons recovered from Barrio Azteca Members in Ciudad Juarez, Mexico

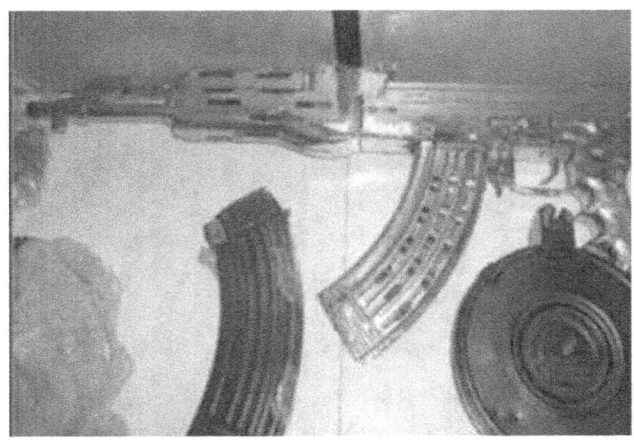

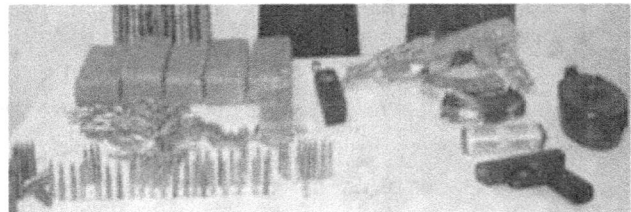

Source: ATF

- In November 2010, a US Navy Seal from San Diego and two others were arrested in Colorado for smuggling at least 18 military issued machine guns and 14 other firearms from Iraq and Afghanistan into the United States for sale and shipment to Mexico, according to open source reporting.[48]

Gang members are employing countermeasures to monitor, intercept, and target law enforcement, sometimes with elaborate weapons and devices.

- In February 2010, a Riverside County gang task force officer in California was nearly killed when suspected members of a White Supremacist gang rigged a zip gun on a gang task force security fence to discharge if anyone entered

Figure 18. Zip gun attached to the fence of a Gang Task Force in Hemet, CA

Source: ATF

their property (see Figure 20). In December 2009, the same group staged a natural gas explosion at their property intended for law enforcement entering the premises.[49]

Gangs and White Collar Crime

NGIC reporting indicates that gangs are becoming more involved in white collar crime, including identity theft, bank fraud, credit card fraud, money laundering, fencing stolen goods, counterfeiting, and mortgage fraud, and are recruiting members who possess those skill sets. Law enforcement officials nationwide indicate that many gangs in their jurisdiction are involved in some type of white collar crime.

- NGIC reporting indicates that the Bloods, Crips, Gangster Disciples, Vice Lords, Latin Kings, Mexican Mafia, Sureños, Norteños, La Nuestra Familia, Texas Syndicate, Aryan Brotherhood, various OMG and Asian gangs, and neighborhood-based gangs are engaging in white collar crime.

Many gang members are engaging in counterfeiting because of its low risks and high financial rewards.

Gang Members Targeting Law Enforcement Vehicles for Weapons

In 2009, suspected gang members in Broward County and West Palm Beach, Florida burglarized nearly a dozen marked and unmarked law enforcement vehicles stealing firearms, ballistic vests, and police identification.

Source: FBI-NGIC, "Gangs Targeting Law Enforcement for Weapons and Equipment Theft; Intelligence Bulletin; 21 December 2009

- In July 2010, a Florencia 13 gang member in Los Angeles was arrested for operating a lab from his home that manufactured pirated video games.[50]

- In April 2010, a member of the East Coast Crips was arrested in Los Angeles, California, for the sale of counterfeit goods and drug trafficking at a clothing store he co-owned. Police confiscated 824 counterfeit items from the store worth $43,762.[51]

Gang members are laundering profits from criminal activities such as drug trafficking and prostitution, through front companies such music businesses, beauty shops, auto repair shops, law firms, and medical offices.

- Members of the Black Guerilla Family in Maryland used pre-paid retail debit cards as virtual currency inside Maryland prisons to purchase drugs and further the gangs' interests, according to August 2010 open source reporting.[52]

Some gangs, such as the Bloods and Gangster Disciples, are committing sophisticated mortgage fraud schemes by purchasing properties with the intent to receive seller assistance loans and, ultimately retain the proceeds from the loans, or to comingle illicit funds through mortgage payments. Gang members are also exploiting vulnerabilities in the banking and mortgage industries for profit.

- According to open source reporting, in April 2009, members of the Bloods in San Diego, California were charged with racketeering and mortgage fraud.[53]

Law Enforcement Actions and Resources

Gang units and task forces are a vital component in targeting gangs and have played a substantial role in mitigating gang activity in a number of US communities. The majority of NGIC law enforcement partners report that their agency has or participates in a gang task force, and most utilize a gang database to track and monitor gang members in their jurisdictions. There are 168 FBI Violent Gang Task Forces in the United States, Puerto Rico, and the US Virgin Islands. In addition, ATF operates 31 Violent Crime Impact Teams (VCIT) and ICE operates eight Operation Community Shield (OCS) Initiatives nationwide (see Appendix C). The collaboration and coordination of federal, state, and local law enforcement agencies has resulted in a number of successes involving gang suppression efforts.

NGIC law enforcement partners in at least 107 jurisdictions report that law enforcement action has resulted in a decrease of gangs or gang activity in their region.

- In March 2011, officials from DHS, CBP, ICE, ATF, and local San Diego police were involved in the arrest of over 67 gang members and associates for drugs and cross-border crimes in the San Diego, California area. Operation Allied Shield III, a part of a San Diego County initiative to focus on prevention, detection, and suppression of crimes in areas impacted by border-related crime, aimed to seize drugs and weapons and to identify and observe gang members in a proactive way.[54]

- In March 2011, 35 leaders, members, and associates of the Barrio Azteca gang in Texas were charged in a federal indictment for various counts of racketeering, murder, drug offenses, money laundering, and obstruction of justice. Ten subjects were charged with the March 2010 murders of a US Consulate employee, her husband, and the husband of another consulate employee, in Juarez, Mexico.[55]

- In February 2011, FBI, ATF, ICE, and DHS, and numerous state and local officials charged 41 gang members and associates from several different gangs in five districts with multiple offenses, including racketeering conspiracy, murder, drug and gun trafficking. The indictment involved members from the Click Clack gang in Kansas City, Missouri; the Colonias Chiques gang in Los Angeles; the Sureno 13 and San Chucos gangs in Las Vegas; MS-13 in Washington; and 13 Tri-City Bomber members and associates in the McAllen, Texas area.[56]

Outlook

Street, prison, and motorcycle gang membership and criminal activity continues to flourish in US communities where gangs identify opportunities to control street level drug sales, and other profitable crimes. Gangs will not only continue to defend their territory from rival gangs, but will also increasingly seek to diversify both their membership and their criminal activities in recognition of potential financial gain. New alliances between rival gangs will likely form as gangs suspend their former racial ideologies in pursuit of mutual profit. Gangs will continue to evolve and adapt to current conditions and law enforcement tactics, diversify their criminal activity, and employ new strategies and technology to enhance their criminal operations, while facilitating lower-risk and more profitable schemes, such as white collar crime.

The expansion of communication networks, especially in wireless communications and the Internet, will allow gang members to form associations and alliances with other gangs and criminal organizations—both domestically and internationally—and enable gang members to better facilitate criminal activity and enhance their criminal operations discreetly without the physical interfacing once necessary to conduct these activities.

Changes in immigrant populations, which are susceptible to victimization and recruitment by gangs, may have the most profound effect on street gang membership. Continued drug trafficking-related violence along the US Southwest border could trigger increased migration of Mexicans and Central Americans into the United States and, as such, provide a greater pool of victims, recruits, and criminal opportunities for street gangs as they seek to profit from the illegal drug trade, alien smuggling, and weapons trafficking. Likewise, increased gang recruitment of youths among the immigrant population may result in an increase in gang membership and gang-related violence in a number of regions.

Street gang activity and violence may also increase as more dangerous gang members are released early from prison and re-establish their roles armed with new knowledge and improved techniques. Prison gang members, already an ideal target audience for radicalization, may expand their associations with foreign gang members or radical criminal organizations, both inside correctional institutions and in the community upon their release.

Gang members armed with high-powered weapons and knowledge and expertise acquired from employment in law enforcement, corrections, or the military may pose an increasing nationwide threat, as they employ these tactics and weapons against law enforcement officials, rival gang members, and civilians.

Globalization, socio-political change, technological advances, and immigration will result either in greater gang expansion and gang-related crime or displace gang members as they search for criminal opportunities elsewhere. Stagnant or poor economic conditions in the United States, including budget cuts in law enforcement, may undercut gang dismantlement efforts and encourage gang expansion as police agencies redirect their resources and disband gang units and taskforces, as reported by a large number of law enforcement agencies.

Maps. Gang Presence in the United States

MAP 1. US NATIONWIDE GANG PRESENCE

UNCLASSIFIED
Nationwide Gang Presence by County, 2010
Gang Members (County estimates)
40,000 and above
10,000 - 24,999
5,000 - 9,999
1,000 - 4,999
less than 1,000
No reporting
Alaska
Hawaii
Chicago Area
Puerto Rico
UNCLASSIFIED

Top 10 Counties in United States				
County	Field Office	Street Gang Members	Motorcycle Gang Members	Total Gang Members*
Los Angeles, California	Los Angeles	68,001	207	68,208
Cook, Illinois	Chicago	59,876	249	60,125
San Bernardino, California	Los Angeles	40,377	181	40,558
Fresno, California	Sacramento	24,376	106	24,482
Hennepin, Minnesota	Minneapolis	19,626	152	19,778
Essex, New Jersey	Newark	17,001	89	17,090
Miami-Dade, Florida	Miami	16,846	38	16,884
Wayne, Michigan	Detroit	15,875	341	16,216
Salt Lake, Utah	Salt Lake City	15,180	194	15,374
Clark, Nevada	Las Vegas	15,125	38	15,163
OTHER COUNTIES		848,061	42,509	890,570
TOTAL		1,140,344	44,508	1,184,852

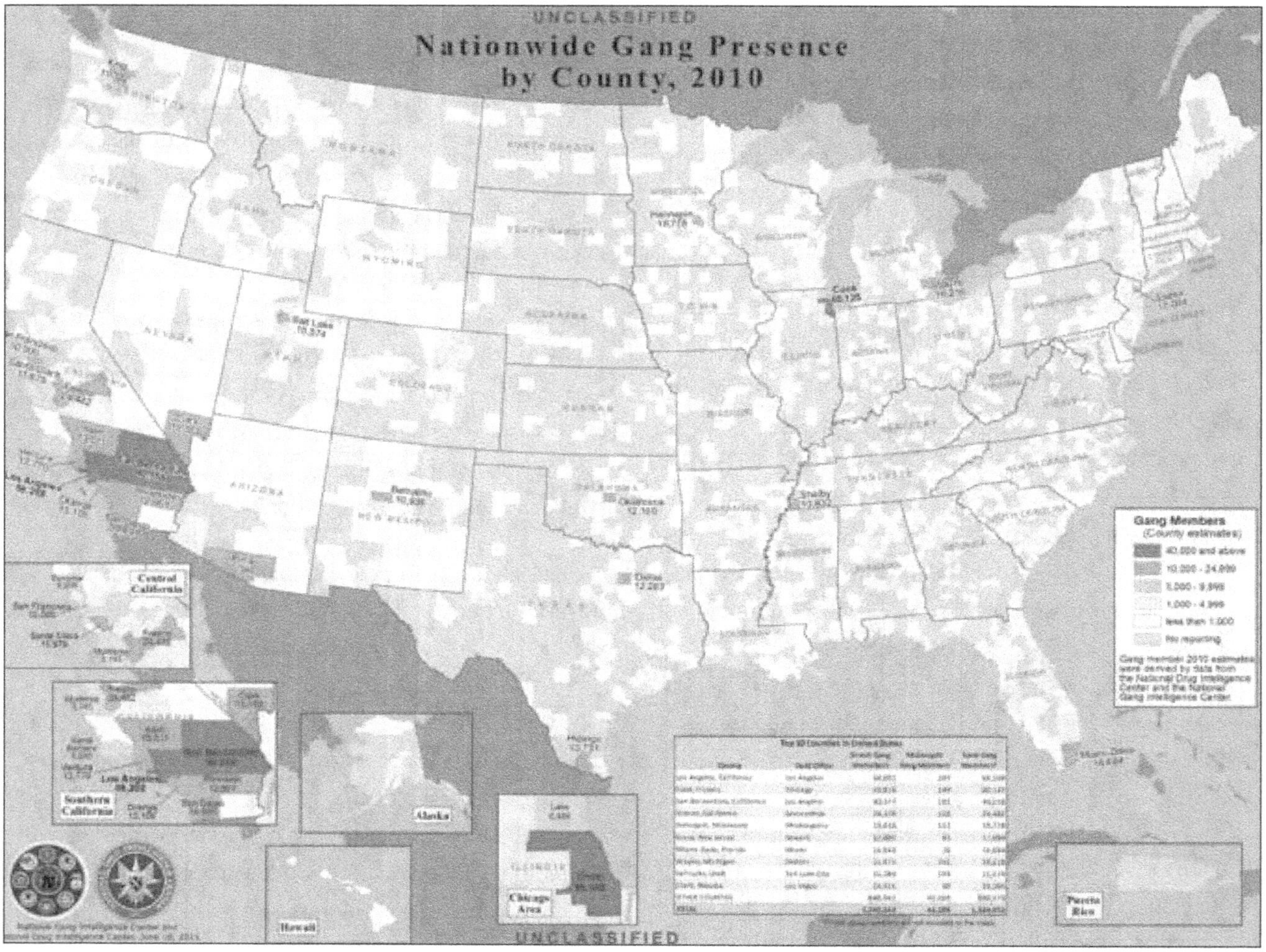

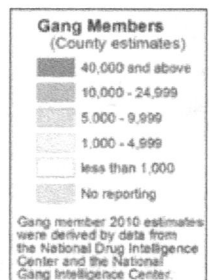

Gang Members
(County estimates)
40,000 and above
10,000 - 24,999
5,000 - 9,999
1,000 - 4,999
less than 1,000
No reporting
Gang member 2010 estimates were derived by data from the National Drug Intelligence Center and the National Gang Intelligence Center.

MAP 2. WEST REGION

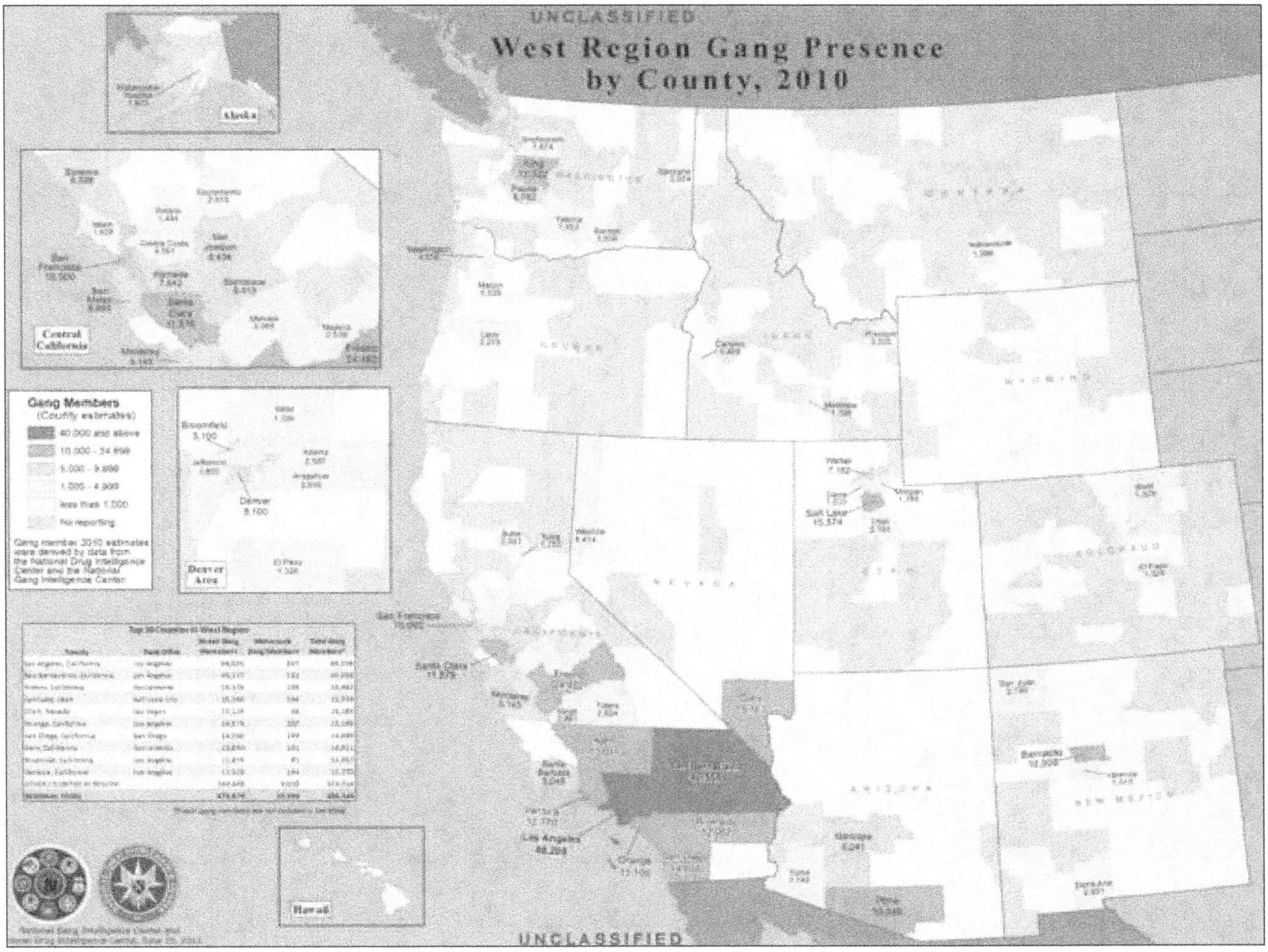

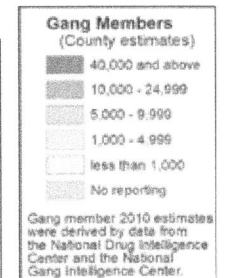

MAP 3. SOUTH CENTRAL REGION

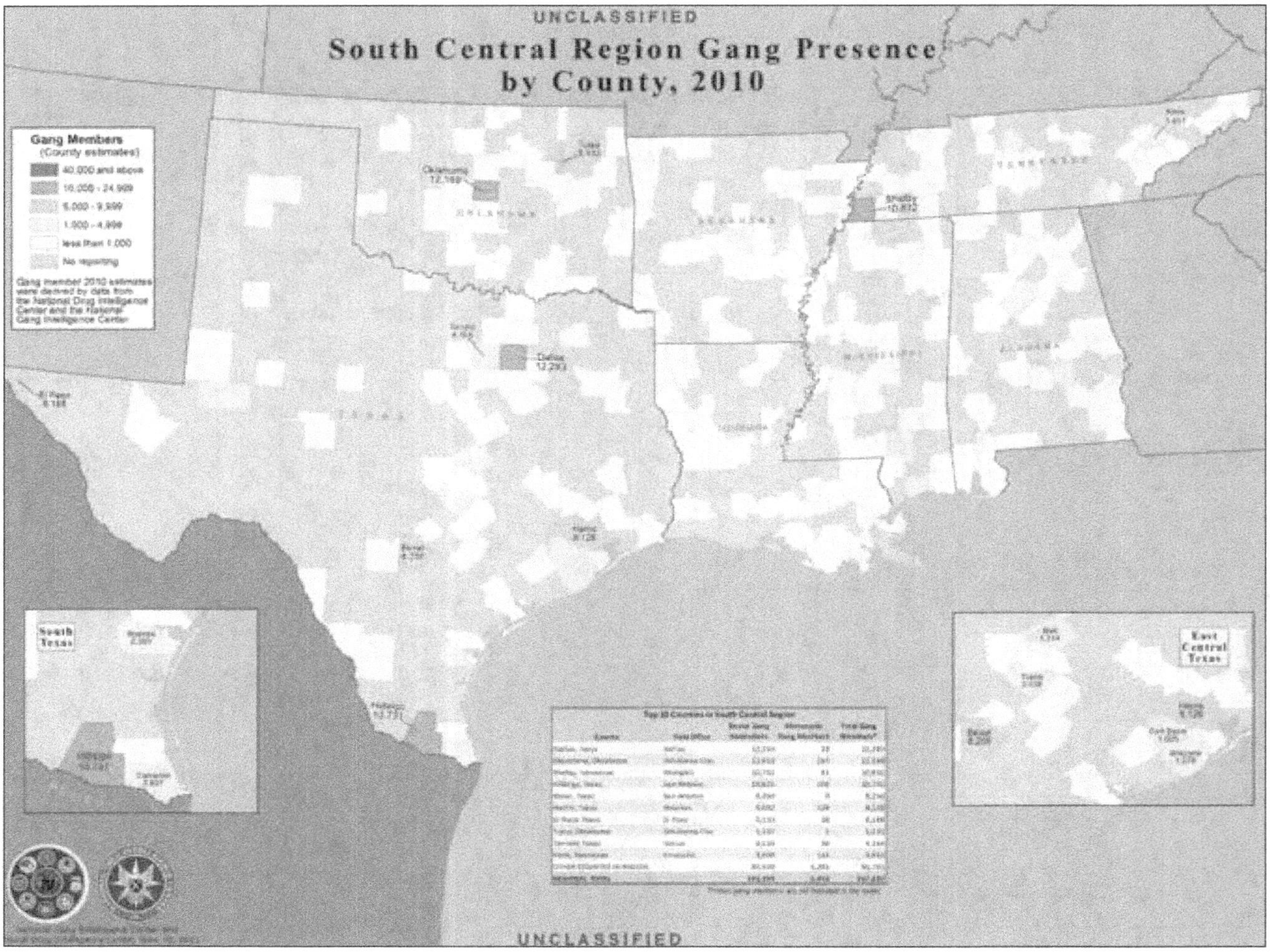

UNCLASSIFIED

South Central Region Gang Presence by County, 2010

UNCLASSIFIED

Top 10 Counties in South Central Region			
County	Field Office	Street Gang Members	Motorcycle Gang Members	Total Gang Members*
Dallas, Texas	Dallas	12,336	23	12,283
Oklahoma, Oklahoma	Oklahoma City	12,012	167	12,169
Shelby, Tennessee	Memphis	10,751	81	10,832
Hidalgo, Texas	San Antonio	10,625	106	10,731
Bexar, Texas	San Antonio	8,250	0	8,250
Harris, Texas	Houston	8,001	124	8,136
El Paso, Texas	El Paso	6,150	38	6,188
Tulsa, Oklahoma	Oklahoma City	6,127	5	6,132
Tarrant, Texas	Dallas	4,326	38	4,364
Knox, Tennessee	Knoxville	3,500	151	3,651
OTHER COUNTIES IN REGION		80,500	1,201	81,701
REGIONAL TOTAL		161,293	1,944	167,237

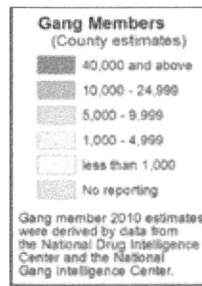

Gang Members
(County estimates)

- 40,000 and above
- 10,000 - 24,999
- 5,000 - 9,999
- 1,000 - 4,999
- less than 1,000
- No reporting

Gang member 2010 estimates were derived by data from the National Drug Intelligence Center and the National Gang Intelligence Center.

MAP 4. NORTH CENTRAL REGION

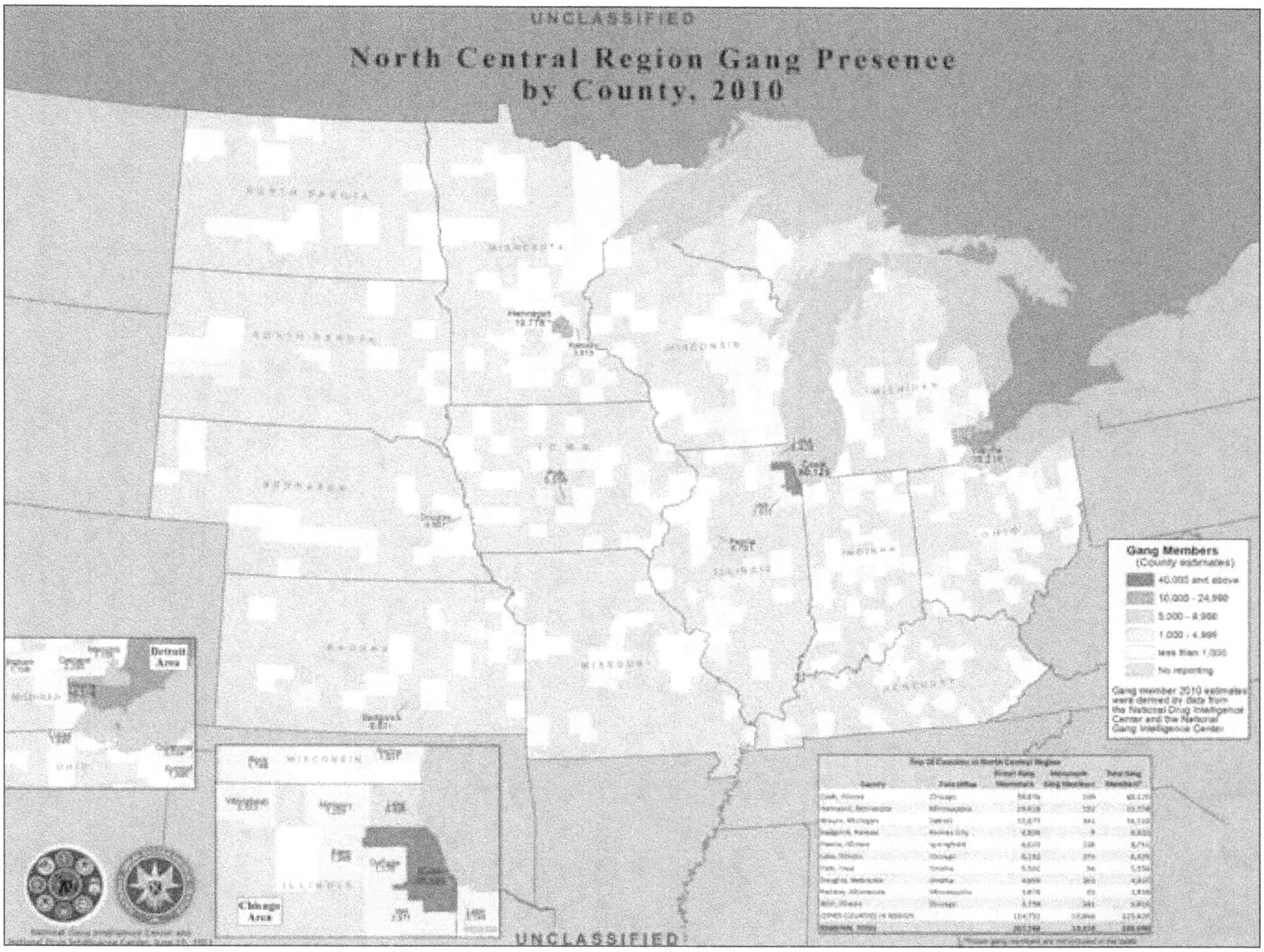

Top 10 Counties in North Central Region				
County	Field Office	Street Gang Members	Motorcycle Gang Members	Total Gang Members*
Cook, Illinois	Chicago	59,876	349	60,129
Hennepin, Minnesota	Minneapolis	19,626	152	19,778
Wayne, Michigan	Detroit	15,875	341	16,216
Sedgwick, Kansas	Kansas City	6,826	5	6,831
Peoria, Illinois	Springfield	6,625	126	6,751
Lake, Illinois	Chicago	6,232	174	6,406
Polk, Iowa	Omaha	5,502	54	5,556
Douglas, Nebraska	Omaha	4,609	203	4,807
Ramsey, Minnesota	Minneapolis	1,876	43	1,919
Will, Illinois	Chicago	3,730	161	3,921
OTHER COUNTIES IN REGION		114,252	10,868	125,620
REGIONAL TOTAL		247,246	12,374	260,040

*Those gang members are not included in the total.

Gang Members (County estimates)

- 40,000 and above
- 10,000 - 24,999
- 5,000 - 9,999
- 1,000 - 4,999
- less than 1,000
- No reporting

Gang member 2010 estimates were derived by data from the National Drug Intelligence Center and the National Gang Intelligence Center.

MAP 5. SOUTHEAST REGION

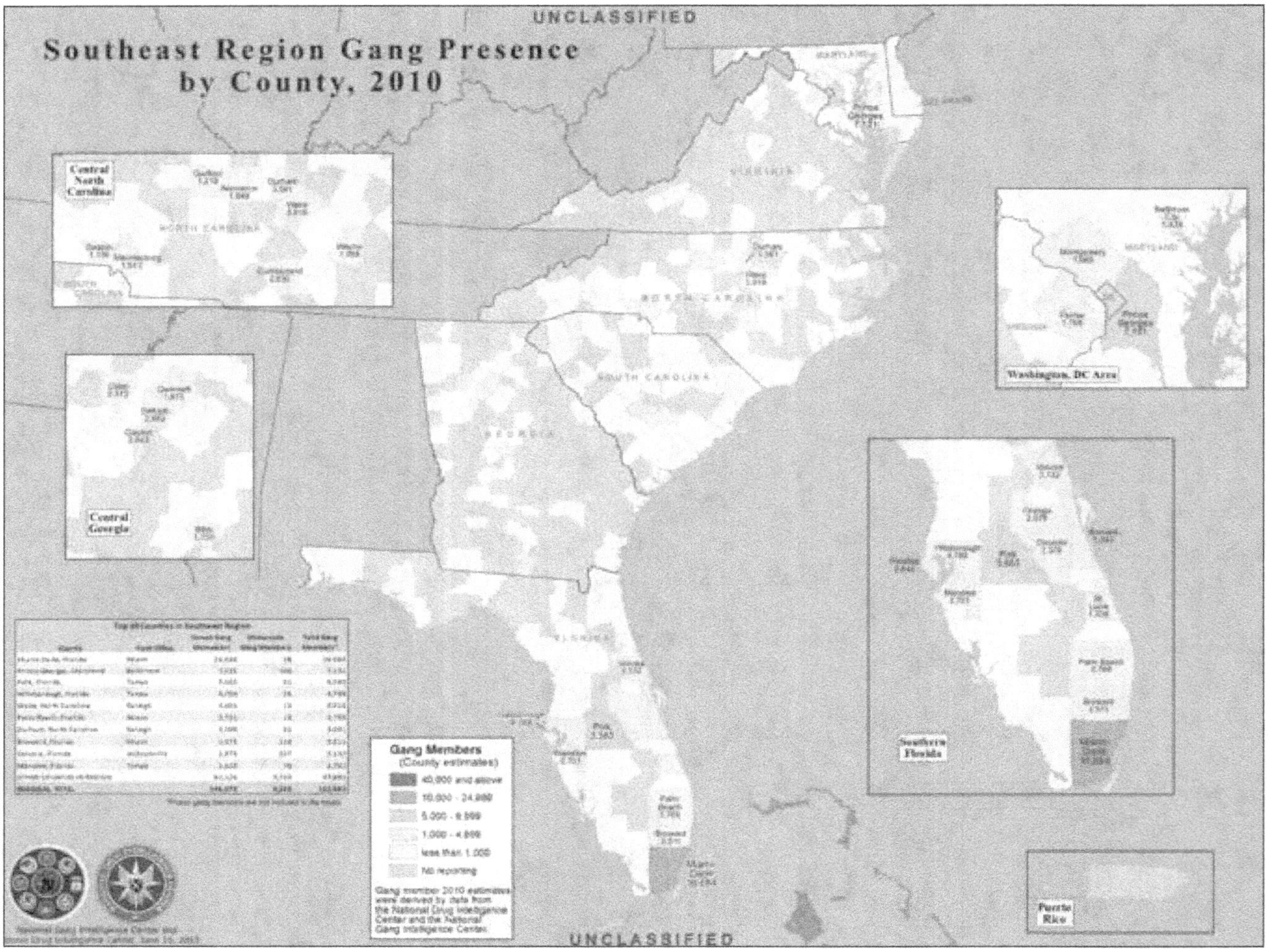

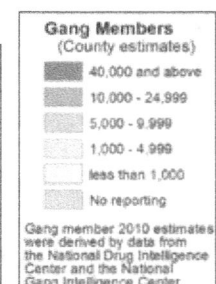

Top 10 Counties in Southeast Region		Street Gang Members	Motorcycle Gang Members	Total Gang Members
County	Field Office			
Miami-Dade, Florida	Miami	14,646	58	14,684
Prince George, Maryland	Baltimore	7,025	108	7,131
Polk, Florida	Tampa	5,932	51	5,483
Hillsborough, Florida	Tampa	4,730	38	4,788
Wake, North Carolina	Raleigh	3,903	15	3,918
Palm Beach, Florida	Miami	3,751	18	3,769
Durham, North Carolina	Raleigh	3,500	51	3,541
Broward, Florida	Miami	3,375	136	3,511
Volusia, Florida	Jacksonville	2,875	257	3,132
Manatee, Florida	Tampa	2,625	78	2,703
OTHER COUNTIES IN REGION		92,126	5,739	97,865
REGIONAL TOTAL		145,075	6,589	152,664

Gang Members
(County estimates)

- 40,000 and above
- 10,000 - 24,999
- 5,000 - 9,999
- 1,000 - 4,999
- less than 1,000
- No reporting

Gang member 2010 estimates were derived by data from the National Drug Intelligence Center and the National Gang Intelligence Center.

MAP 6. NORTHEAST REGION

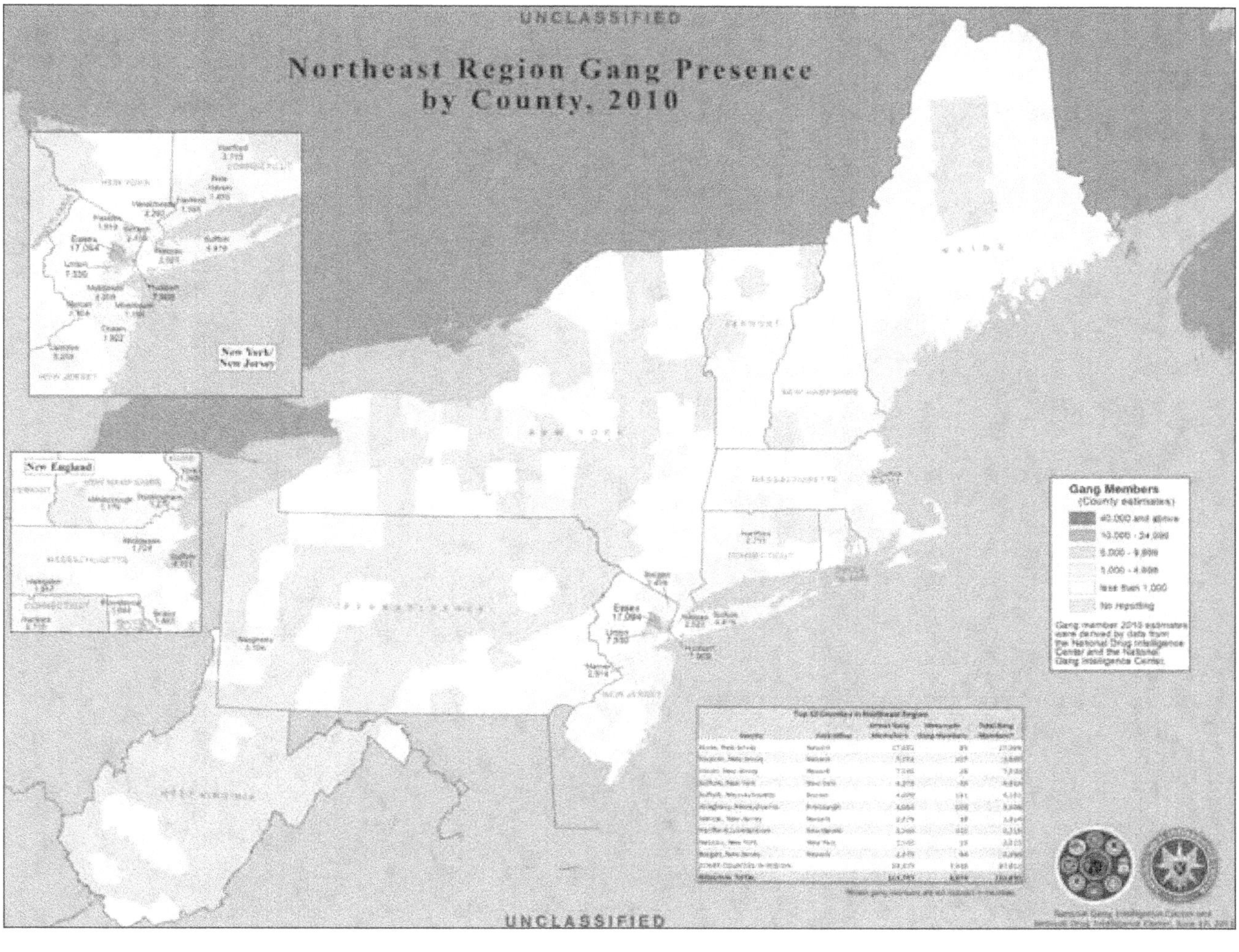

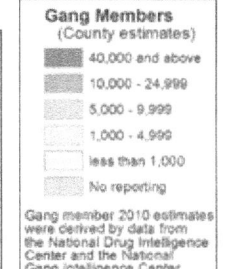

Northeast Region Gang Presence by County, 2010

Top 10 Counties in Northeast Region		Street Gang Members	Motorcycle Gang Members	Total Gang Members*
County	Field Office			
Essex, New Jersey	Newark	17,001	93	17,094
Hudson, New Jersey	Newark	7,752	157	7,906
Union, New Jersey	Newark	7,502	28	7,530
Suffolk, New York	New York	6,374	43	6,418
Suffolk, Massachusetts	Boston	4,000	151	4,151
Allegheny, Pennsylvania	Pittsburgh	3,860	108	3,108
Mercer, New Jersey	Newark	2,879	34	2,914
Hartford, Connecticut	New Haven	2,500	215	2,715
Nassau, New York	New York	2,590	23	2,522
Bergen, New Jersey	Newark	2,375	84	2,498
OTHER COUNTIES IN REGION		59,873	1,936	67,811
REGIONAL TOTAL		116,267	4,878	121,685

Gang Members (County estimates)
- 40,000 and above
- 10,000 - 24,999
- 5,000 - 9,999
- 1,000 - 4,999
- less than 1,000
- No reporting

Gang member 2010 estimates were derived by data from the National Drug Intelligence Center and the National Gang Intelligence Center

MAP 7. FBI UNIFORM CRIME REPORT (UCR) VIOLENT CRIME, 2009

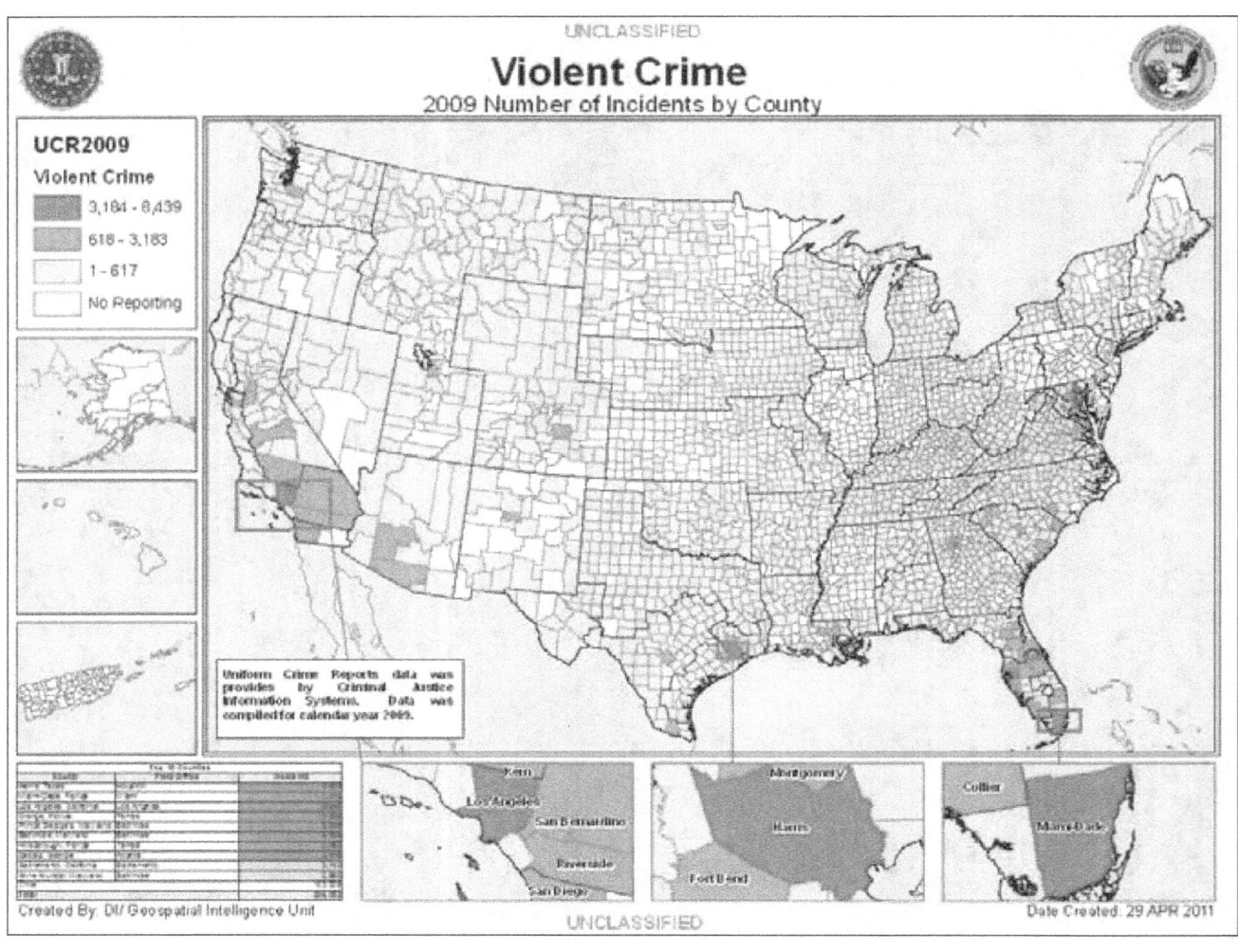

APPENDIX A. Gangs by State

ALABAMA
31st Street Mob
33rd Street Posse
400 Block
4th Ward Bloods
Alberta City Boys
Alpha Tau Omega
Aryan Brotherhood
Avenue Piru Gangsters Bandaleros
Bandidos MC
Bay Boys
Black Cherry 8 Balls
Black Gangster Disciples
Black Mafia Family
Black Pistons MC
Bloods Boom Squad
Brown Pride
Central Park Bloods
Central Park Boys
Collegeville Posse
Corner Boys Crips
Devils Disciples MC
Eastside Bloods
Ensley Town Killers
Evergreen Bottom Boys
Gad Town Klowns
Gangsta G's
Gangster Disciples
Ghettie Boyz
Give No Fucks
Green Acres Crips
Hazel Green Boys
Hells Lovers MC
Imperial Gangster Disciples
Insane Gangster Disciples

Juggalos
La Familia
La Quemada
Latin Kings
Latino Bloods Crips
Little Trouble Makers
Los Bolinos
Los Zetas
Lovemans Village Posse
Lynch Mob
Malditos 13
Melos 13
Northside Bloods
Northsiders 62 Po Boys
On Fire Boys
On Fire Girls
Outcast MC
Pistoleros MC
Outlaws MC
Pratt Boys
Riley Boys
Seven Deadly Sins
Sherman Heights Posse
Sin City Disciples MC
Six Deuce Brims
Smithfield Posse
Southern Brotherhood
Southside Cyclones
Southside Locos
Southside Youngsters
Sur-13
T Dub
Tango Blast
Technical Knockout
Titusville Posse

Toney Project Boys
Trap Boys
Trap Girls
Tribe MC
United Together Forever
Vatos Locos
Vice Hill Posse
Vice Lords
View Mob
Westside Crips
Wheels of Soul MC
Wylam Boys

ALASKA
50150 Crips
88 Street Crips
Almighty Latin King Nation
Almighty Vice Lord Nation
Altadena Crip Gangster
American Front
Aryan Brotherhood
Baby Hamo Tribe
Black Gangster Disciples
Blackwood Mafia
Chaos Drama Family
Combat Crips
Compton Swamp Crips
Deuce
Faceside Bloods
Fam Bam
Franklin Family Piru
Fresno Bulldogs
Full Time Criminals
Gangster Disciples
Goonies For Life

Hamo Tribe

Hells Angels MC

Hmong Nation Society

Hollow Tip Crew

Iceberg Clique

Juvenile Delinquents

Korrupt(ed) Crew

Laos Oriental Soldiers

Laotian Blood Killers

Laotian Thugz

Locc Down Crips

Loco Latin Crips

Los Malditos

MS-13

Member of Blood

Menace of Destruction

Mongolian Boys Society

Mountain View Crips

Murder Mob

Northside Damu

Outlawz

Peckerwoods

Real 'Bout It Individuals

Royal Samoan Posse

Samoan Dynasty

Sons of Samoa

Soulja Crew

Southside Mesa

Sureños

The Family

The Low Lifes

Tiny Rascals Gang

Tongang Crip Gang

Top Notch Ballers

Uso 4 Life

Uso Squad

Westside City Crips

Westside Inland Empire Projects

Yellow Oriental Troop

Young Gangsta Niggas

ARIZONA

"A" Mountain Crips

10th Ave JP Crips

12th Ave Crips

29th Street Bloods

36th Street Vista Bloods

36th Street Vista Chicanos

4th Ave Crips

Aryan Brotherhood

Barrio Anita

Barrio Centro

Barrio Chicano Southside

Barrio Hollywood

Barrio Libre

Barrio Loco

Barrio Nuevo Locos

Barrio Savaco

Bilby Street Crips

Black Rags

Duce Nine Crips

Eastside Bloods

Eastside Crips

Eastside Maria Crips

Eastside Torrance

Folk Nation

Gangster Disciples

Grandale

Hells Angels MC

Hollywood Soma

Juggalos

Jollyville Crips

La Tusa

La Victoria Locos

Little Town

Little Town Crips

Locos Bloodline

Manzanita Lynch Mob Crips

Maryvale Gangsta Crips

Mau Mau

Mexican Mafia

Midvale Park Bloods

Mission Manor Park Bloods

Mongols

New Mexican Mafia

Northside Chicanos

Northside White Pride

Okie Town

Old Mexican Mafia

Old Pascua

Peckerwoods

Skinheads

Sons of Hell

South Palo Verde Bloods

South Park Family Gangsters

Southeast Hustler Bloods

Southside Boyz

Southside Brown Pride

Southside Harbor City

Southside Posse Bloods

Sureños

Trekell Park Crips

Varrio Loco

V-12 Bloods

Vagos MC

Vindlanders

West Mesa

West Ross Street Piru

Western Hills Posse Bloods

Westside Brown Pride

Wet Back Power

Warrior Society

Western Hills Bloods

ARKANSAS

Bandidos MC

Blood

Crips

Folk Nation

Outlaws MC

People Nation

Sons of Silence MC

Wheels of Soul MC

CALIFORNIA

18th St

159th Avenue

17th St

38th Avenue Locos

38th Street

415 Kumi

49 St hustler Crips

5/9 Brims

51st Avenue locos

51st St locos

A Street

AC Acorn

Acre Boys

Al Capone

Aryan Brotherhood

Asian Boyz

Asian Crips

Asian Insane Boys

Asian Street Walkers

Asian Warriors

Atascadero 13

AVE 39

AVE 51

AVE 53

Aztec Tribe Cholos

Azusa 13

B Street

Bahala Na' Barkada

Bakersfield Bastards MC

Barrio San Juan 13

Barrio Cathedral City

Barrio Eastside

Barrio Pobre

Barrio San Juan

Barrio Small Town

Brown Brotherhood

Brown Crowd Locos

Barrio Central Vallejo

Black Guerilla Family

Block Boys

Blue Team

Blvd Crips

Bolen

Border Brothers

Bratz

Brick Block Crips

Broderick Boys

Brown Brotherhood

Brown Life Familia

Brown Pride Soldiers

Brown Pride Soldiers 13

Brown Pride Sureño

Browns Town

Bulldogs

Burger Team

Calle Ocho (8th street)

Campbell Village Gangsters

Campos Ramos Locos

Canta Ranas 13

Carmelas 13

Carps

Central Vallejo Clicka

Chankla Bulldogs

Chino Sinners

City Heights Trece Juniors

Clairemont Locos

Coachella Tiny Locos

CoCo County Boys

Cold Nigga Mafia

Colonia Bakers

Compton Varrio Tortilla Flats

Corona Varrio Locos

Country Boy Crips

COVINA 13

Crazy Brothers Clan

Crazy Brown Norteños

Crazy Fucking Mexicans

Crazy Krooks

Crazy Royal Kings

Crow Village

Cudahy 13

Cut Throat Mob

Davis Street Locos

Dead End Street

Death Crowd 13

Del Sol

Delhi Alley Boys

Desperados MC

Dirty Thirties

Dog Soldiers

Dreamhomes

Droppin Niggas Instantly

Down To Scrap Krew

East Coast Crips

Eastbound Loco

Eastside Familia

Eastside Longos

Eastside Rivas

Eastside SD El Cajon Locos

El Hoyo Palmas

EL Monte Flores

Elm St Watts

Eastside Montalvo

Exotic Foreign City Crips

Family Affiliated Irish Mafia Fain

Familia Hispana

Farmerside Bulldogs

Florencia 13

Four Corner Block Crips

Fresnecks Ftroop

Fuck My Enemies

Fuck the World

Gardenview Locos

Gas Team

Gateway Posse Crips

Ghetto Assassins

Ghostown

Goleta 13

H Street

Hard Side Clique

Hard Times

Hawaiian Gardens 13

Hells Angels MC

Highly Insane Criminals

Hispanic Kings

Homicidal Family

Hoodlum Family

Hop Sing Boyz

Humboldt

Humboldt County Gangsters

Imperials

Indian Pride

Inglewood Family Gangster

Inglewood Trece

Insane Crips

Insane Viet Thugz

Jackson Terrace

Jamaican Mafia Family

Juggalos

Kansas Street

Kings Of Cali MC

Krazy Ass Samoans

Krazy Assassins

Kumi

La Nuestra Familia

LB Suicidal Punks

Lennox

Lincoln Park Piru

Lincoln Town Sureños

Linda Vista 13

Lo Mob

Logan 30ta

Logan Heights

Logan Red Steps

Loma Bakers

Lomita Village 70's

Long Beach Locos

Lorenzo Team

Los Marijuanas Smokers

Los Nietos 13

Los Padrinos

Low Profile Kings

Lo Boys

Lunatics On Crack

Lynwood Dukes

Mac Mafia

Manor Dro Boyz

Manor Park Gangsters

Marijuana Locos

Mayfair Santa Rosa Criminals

Mexican Klan Locos

Mexican Mafia

Mexican Pride 13

Midcity Stoners

Midtown Proyectos

Mission Bay Locos

Mitchel Street Norteños

Mob Squad

Mob To Kill

Molochs

Mongols MC

Mountain View Sureños

MS-13

National City Locos

Nazi Low Riders

Neighborhood Crips

Nip Killer Squad

Nipomo 13 Norte

North Town Stoners

Northern Riders

Northern Structure

Northside Hayward

Northside Indio

Northside Longos

Nuestra Raza

Nutty Side Paramount

Oaktown Crips

Oceano 13

O-hood Crips

Okie Bakers

Old Town National City

Olivo Bulldogs

Oriental Boy Soldiers

Oriental Boys

Oriental Killer Boys

Oriental Lazy Boys

Orphans

Otay	Skinheads	Varrio Concord Norte
Palm City	Skyline Piru	Varrio Northside
Paradise Hills Locos	So Gate Tokers	Varrio Nueva Estrada
Paso Robles 13	Sobrante Park	Varrio Simi Valley
Peckerwoods	Solano Side	Varrio Bakers
Public Enemy Number One (PENI)	Sons of Samoa	Varrio Chula Vista
Pierpont Rats	Sotel 13	Varrio Coachella Rifa
Pierpont-Ventura	South Gate Smokers	Varrio Coachella Rifa 52
Playa Larga	South Vietnam	Varrio Coachella Rifa 53
Pomona 12th Street	Southeast Locos	Varrio Encanto Locos
Power of Vietnamese	Southern Locos Gangsters 13	Varrio Grinfas
Puente 13	Southside Bakers	Varrio Horseshoe
Pure Mexican Raza	Southside Criminals	Varrio Locos
Puro Raza Loco	Southside Huntington Beach	Varrio Meadow Fair
Puro Varrio Campo	Southside Indio	Varrio Mecca Rifa
Quiet Assassins	Southside Playboys	Varrio Mountain View
Quiet Village 13	Southside Players	Varrio Norwalk 13
Quince Southside Locos	Southside Whittier 13	Varrio Nuevo Coachella
Red Team	Spring Valley Locos	Varrio Oasis Rifa
Res Boys	Squeeze Team	Varrio Palmas Gang
Ridezilla	Sucidals Sunny Block Crips	Varrio Penn West
Rockcreek	Sunnyvale Sur Trece	Varrio South Garden
Rollin 20 Crips	Sur Santos Pride	Varrio Sur Rifa
S. Central Locos	Sur Town Locos	Varrio Tamilee Gangsters
Sacramaniacs	Sureño Unidos Trece	Varrio Thermal Rifa
San Dimas Rifa	Sureños Por Vida	Varrio Xechos Locos
San Jose Crazy Crips	Tangas	Vatos Locos
San Jose Grande	Tehachapi 13	Venice 13
San St Paramount	Tiny Rascal Gang	Venice Shoreline Crips
Santa Monica Gang	Tongan For Life	Viet Outlaws
Santa Nita	Top Hatters	Vietnam
Saticoy- Ventura Eastside	Underworld Zilla	Wah Ching
Screamin Demons MC	Untouchables	Walnut Creek 13
Shandon Park Locos 13 Shelltown	USO Squad	Warlord Bloods
Shelltown Gamma	Ventura Avenue Gangsters	West Coast Crips
Sherman Lomas Market Street	Vagos MC	West Covina 13
Sidro	Valinda Flats	West Covina Crips

West Covina MOB
West Drive Locos
West Myrtle Townsend Street
Westside Hustlers
Westside Islanders
Westside Locos
Westside Longos
Westside MOB
Westside Stoners
Wheels of Soul MC
White Power
Whittier
Wicked Minded Sureños
Wicked Minded Sureños 13
Willow Street
Young Crazy Thugs
Young Cutties
Zetas

COLORADO
18th Street
211 Crew
81st Street Crips
American Nazi Party
Bandidos MC
Brown Pride Sureños
Carver Park Crips
Eastside Dukes
Folks
Gallant Knights
Gangster Disciples
GKI 211 Crew Bloods
Hells Angels
Insane Norteños
Juaritos
Kraziest Thugs Around
Los Primer Padres

Mexican Mafia
MS-13
Mongols MC
Murder All Cliques
Norteños
Northside Criminals
Northside Mafia
Oldies 13
Outlaws MC
Paisas
Parkside Varrio
Peckerwoods
Playboys
Sons of Silence MC
Southside Locos
Sureño Desert Empire
Sureños
Two Eleven

CONNECTICUT
Battalion 14
Blake Street Goonies
Bloods
Carmel Street Goons
Charter Oak Crips
Cruel 36 Family
Diablos MC
Eastern Circle Projects 3x
Fairside 2x
G-25
G-27
G-Side Projects
Hells Angels MC
Hill Most Wanted
Hillside 4x
La Familia

Latin Kings and Queens
Manor 5x
MS-13
Netas
Outlaws MC
Solidos
The Ave
Tiny Mami Squad
Tiny Papi Squad
Tre 3x
Tribe 3x
Trinitarios
Ville 2x

DISTRICT OF COLUMBIA
18th Street
Bloods
Crips
Latin Kings
MS-13

DELAWARE
135 Bloods
9 Trey
9 Triggaz
924 Bloods
Anybody Gets It
Bounty Hunter Bloods
Bush Babies
Cash Hoe Murda
Certified Ballina Killers
Crips
Dawg City Piru
East Coast Bloods
Gangster Disciples
Latin Kings
Netas
Ochos

Pagans

South Los

Sur-13

Street Piru Bloods

FLORIDA

1000 Block

103rd St Buck Wild CA Latin Lingo

10th St Gang

110th St Bloods

1200 Block

12th Court Cowboys

13th Avenue Hotboys

13th Street Gang

170 Boyz

181

187

1887

18th Street

20 Deep

21 Gunz

211 Crips

2150 EAP

22nd Street

23rd Street Trail Blazers

24th Street Gang

25 Mafia

27's Puerto Rico PG

2nd Line Goons

300 Block

311 Westside KTP

312 Crips

7414 Gangster Disciples

34th Folk Boys

39th Street Boys

3KN

4 Way Boys

45th St FAM

46 Ave Boyz

5 Deuce Hoover Crips

5 Trey Bloods

5% 386

5020 Peckerwood

5150 Piru Bloods

52 Hoover Crips

551 Crips

58th Ave.

59 Hoover Crips

7 Trey Crips

700 Block

74 Gangster Disciples

7414 Gangster Disciples

8 Tre Crips

8 Trey Gangster Crips

800 Bound

813 Black Gangster Disciples

819 Boys

9 Trey Gangsters

9 Trey Murk Squad Blood

9-Tech Bloods

A&E Bird Gang

Ace Boon Goons

All City Certified Gangstas

Almighty Latin King and Queen Nation

American Nazi Party Anarchist

Anarchist

Any Body Killas

APK Boys

Aryan Brotherhood

Aryan Nation

Barrio Boys

Batchelors

Behind the Plaza Boys

Beruit Snakes

Big Money Posse

Bithlo Bike Crew

Black Angels

Black Flag Mafia

Black Gangster Disciple

Black Mafia

Black MOB

Black P Stone Nation

Black Pines

Black Pistons MC

Black Spade Squad

Black T Mafia

Blue Angel

Blue Devil Gangster Crips

Booker Heights Posse

Border Brothers

Brookhill Hillboys Most Wanted

Brown Pride

Bruise Brothers MC

Buck Block

Camphor Way Boys

Cartel Southside Gansta Crips

Carver Shore Boys

Cash Feenz

CFL Most Wanted

Chicago Bloods

Chico Cracker Klique

Chico's In Action

Click Tight

Clown Boiz Crips

Cold Side Posse

College Park Thugs

Confederate Hammerskins

Corner Boy Mafia

Crazy Brown Boys

Crazy Gangster Disciple

Crazy Insane Disciples	Eureka Garden Goons	Imperial Gangsters
Crazy Killer Zoes	Every Niggas Nightmare	Imperial Kings Inland Empire
Criminal Gangsters	Family of Hustlers	Insane Dragons
Cut Throat Crew/Committee	Flag Street	Insane Gangster Crips
D-BOYZ	Flip Star Crips	Insane Gangster Disciple
Dirty White Boys	Florencia 13	Insane MOB Boys
Down 4 Whatever	Folk	Insane Spanish Lords
Dark Angels	Folk Disciples	International Folk Posse
Darkside Boyz	Folk Nation	International Posse
Deaths Last Clique	For The Warriors	International Posse 13th
Deland Regulators	Front Street Boyz	Island Boys Clique
DeLeon Springs	G Shine Bloods	Jack Boys
Deuce Crips	G Stone Crip	Jensen Beach Clique
Deuce Deuce	G25	Juggalos
Dirty Game	Gangster Killer Bloods	Knock Out Squad
Dirty South Mafia	Gangsta Piru	King Con Sureños
Dirty White Boys	Gangstas For Life	Keep On Spraying
Disciples of Discipline	Gangster Disciples	Ken Knight
Doo Doo Creek	Gangster Imperial Gangsters	Krazy Getdown Boys
Doom Squad	Gangster Prophet	Kruption Boys
Dover Locos	Gangsters 4 Life	Kuntry Boyz
Down For Life	Get Up Kids	La Raza
Down South Florida Boys	Ghostrider Crips	Lady Knock Out Squad
Down South Gangster	Golden Gate Goons	Lakawanna Boys Latin Crew
Downtown Crips	Goyams	Latin Disciples
DRAK BOYS	Grand Park Grape Street Crips	Latin Eagles
Draks	Guardians	Latin Kings
Dred Mafia	Guk-Get Up Kids	Latin Life
East Orlando Warriors	Gun Clap N Crips	Latin Lingo Legacy Mafia
Eastside 9 Trey Gangster Bloods	Hammerskins	Latin Syndicates
Eastside Bloods	Hill Top Boys	Legion of Doom
Eastside Crips	Hoover Crip	Little Altamonte Goons
Eastside Jack Boyz	Hoover Deuce Crips	Little Haiti Bloods
Eastside Piru	Hope Circle Bois	Livingston Dawgs
Eastside Rolling 60's Crips	Hot Boys	Lockhart Boyz
Elm Street Piru Bloods	Hustle Harder	Loco Trece
Eternal Gangster	Imperial Gangster Disciples	Los 27

Los Chicanos	Nuestra Familia	Platoon 187
Los Salidos	Nine Trey Blood	Playboy Crew
Lost Boys	Nine Trey Gangsters	Polk Street Goons
Lusoanderson Boys	Nines Techs & Grenades Norte 14	Port Orange Boys
M.A.C. Crip	Northlake Boys	Power Progress
Mafia Kings	Not Fair Ones	Project Boys
Mafia Street Gangsta Crips	Nuccio Boys	Projects of Vietnam
Main Street Posse	Oak Ridge Jungle Boys	P-Town
Maniac Campbell Disc Ñeta	Oaktown Niggaz	PYC Raw Dawgz
Maniac Gangster Disciples	Oceanway Mafia	Renegades MC
Maniac Latin Disciples	OLD Gang	Ridge Manor Boys
Mascotte City Gangster Folk Nation	One Love Nation	Rollin 20s Crips
Mayan Pride	Orange City Boys	Rollin 30's
Melbourne Town Soldiers	Orange County Gangs 1400 Block	Rolling 60 Crips
Mexican Diplomats	Orange Flag Boys	Rough Riders
Mexican Mafia	Out East Outlaws	Royal Family Ace Clique
Midway Goons	Out of Control Gangster	Salerno Boyz
Milla Southside	Outlaw Crips Outlawz	Satan Disciples
Miller Gangsta Blood	Outlaw Gangster Crips	Satan Gangster Disciples
Miller Set	Outlaws MC	Satanist
MOB Folks	O.V. BOYS	Savage Squad
Mohawk Boys	Oviedo Soldiers	Sex Money Murder Bloods
Moncrief "MCT"	P.O. Boys	Sherwood
Money Mafia	Payback Crips	Shores Boys
Morgan Boys	Pagans MC	Sin City Boyz
Most Hated Brothers	Paisa Palm River Boys	Six Point Crips
Mother Fuckin Goons	Palm City Locals	Skinheads
Money Power Respect	Palmdale	Smooth Fellas
MS-13	Parramore Snakes	So Bout It Boiz
Murda Grove Boys	Paxon Boys	Solo G
Murder Set Bloods	Pearl World	Sons of Silence MC
Murk	People Nation	Southern Pitbulls
Myrtle Avenue	Phantom MC	Southside
Nazi Juggalo	Picketville Hustle House	Southside Bloods
Ñeta	Pine Hills Pimp Boyz	Southside Crips
New Smyrna Beach Boyz	Pine Manor Piru Bloods	Spanish Lords
New York Outlaws	Piru Bloods	St. Lucie Bloods Chicos in Action

Stand and Deliver

Str8drop Gang

Straight Drop

Street Runners

Supreme White Power

Sur-13

Sureños

Swamp Boyz

Tangos

TC Boys

The Fresh Kings

Third World Family

Thunder Cats

Tri-State

Top Shottas

Tre 4

Troop 31 Slum Boys Aryan Nations

Tru Soldiers

Unforgiven

Unforgiven International Posse

United Crip Nation

United King

Unknown Soldiers

Up Top Mafia

Valentine Bloods

Vandalize The Hood

Vagos

Vato Locos

Vice Lord

Victory Boyz

Villa Boyz

Villa Killas

Village Boys

V-Side Gangsters

Warlocks MC

Washington Oaks Goons

Watauga Boys

Watts City Crips

Westside

Westside Chico Boys

Westside Crips

Westside Rolling 60's Crips

Westside Rolling 90's Crips

White Aryan Resistance

White Power

White Pride

Wildside Young Boon Goons

Winter Garden

Wolfpack MC

Woodlands Crew

Woods Boyz

Wynwood

Y-B Zoe Pound

Y-Lo-C

Young Godz

Young Guz

Young Latin Organization

Young Outlaw Gangster Crips

Zellwood Boys

Zoe Mafia

Zoe Mafia Family

Zoe Pound

Zone 1

Zulus MC

GEORGIA

30 Deep

4WB Fourth Ward Boys

All About Cash

All About Finesse

All About Money

Atlanta Blood Gang Squad

ATL Riders

Bang Bang Anywhere Gang

Bank First Play Later

Bethel Towers Crew

Black Pistons MC

BMB Blood Money Boys

Bloods

Campbelton Road Gangsters

Certified Street Niggas

Certified Paper Chasers

Check Gang

Crips

Cross the Track Boys

Da Fam

Dem Franchise Boys

Deadly Killer Click

DTS Dogwood Trap Starts

Fuck Being Broke

Gangsta Azz Nicca

Gangster Disciples

GD 74

Gett Money Play Later Click

Guapaholic Hard Times 13

Gwalla Boys

Hard Times

Hot Boy Click

Insane Gangster Disciples

Irwin Street Gorillas

James Gang MC

Merk Squad

Most Dangerous Click

Niggas Bout Action

Niggas for Life

No Mercy/ Trained to Go

Oakland City Posse

Outcast MC

Outlaws MC

Partners of the Struggle

Pittsburgh Jack Boys

RACK Crew
Raised on Cleveland
Rollin 20's Bloods
Rollin 60's Crips
Runts
Simpson Road Gangsters
Stealing Everything (SIMPSET)
Sureños
Sur-13
Southside 13
Sur King Locos
Ten Little Niggas
Trained to Go
Vagos
Vatos Locos
Vice Lords
White Boi Gang
Young Block Boys
Young Choppa Fam
Young Committed Partnas
Young Cushman Boys
Young Get Money Gangsters
Young Gunna Click
Young Money Makers
Young Niggas Get Money
Young Paper Chasers
Young Crew
YSet/ Y3/ Sak Takerz

HAWAII
Vagos MC

IDAHO
Bandidos MC
Brothers Speed MC
Mexican Mafia

Northside Big Tyme
Nuestra Familia
Russian Gangs
Vagos MC
Westside 18th Street
Westside Loma Locos

ILLINOIS
12th St Players
Almighty Popes
Ambrose
Black Disciples
Black Gangster Disciples
Black P Stones
Black Pistons MC
Folks Nation
Gangster Disciples
Hells Angels
Hobo's Imperial Gangsters
Insane Dragons
Jivers Jousters
Krazy Get Down Boys
La Raza
Latin Counts
Latin Kings
Latin Saints
Latin Souls
Leafland Street Boys
Latins Out of Control
Maniac Latin Disciples
Mickey Cobra's
Outlaws MC
Party People
People Nation
Popes
Satan Disciples
Satin Disciples

Simon City Rollers
Sons of Silence
Spanish Cobras
Sur-13
Two Six
Vice Lords
Wheels of Soul MC

INDIANA
13's Sureños
14's Norteños
18th Street
American Mexican Gangster
Aryan Brotherhood
Back Pistons MC
Black Angels
Black Gangster Disciples
Black P Stones
Bloods
BPS 13
Brown Pride Gang
Buffalo Soldiers
Click Clack
Cloven Hoofs MC
Code Red
Code Red
Rollin's 20's Crips
Cossacks
D-Boyz
Devil Disciples
Diablos MC
Dirty White Boys
Gangster Disciples
Goons Squad
Grim Reapers MC
Haughville Syndicate
Hells Angels MC

Insane Gangster Disciples
Jimtown Boys
Kentuckiana Gunslingers
Latin Kings
Latino Riders
Locos 18
Luchiana Boyz
Mad Dog MC
Mexican Mafia
Midnight Riders MC
Milwaukee Iron
Mistic Dragons
Money Over Bitches
Mongols MC
MS-13
Murda Squad
Naptown Riders
Norteño
Northside Vatos Locos
Outlaws MC
Peace Stones
Pop It Off Boys
Pussy and Cash
Ratchet Boyz
Rebel Cause
Righteous Riders
Savages and White Boys
Saxon Knights
Sons of Silence MC
Stone Drifters
Straight Edge
Sur-13
The Cool Kids
Vice Lords
Westside Crew
Wheels of Soul MC
Zoe Pound

IOWA
18th Street
319 Crew
7 Deuces
Ambrose
Aryan Brotherhood
Aryan Nation
Aztec Kings
Black Cross
Black Disciples
Black Gangster Disciples
Black Gangsters
Black Mafia
Black P Stones
Black Panthers
Black P-Stone Nation
Black Soul Block Burners
Blackstone Rangers
Bloods
Bogus Boys
Branded Breed MC
Carney Pride
Chosen Few MC
Church of the Creator
Church of the New Song
Code Red
Custom Riders MC
Crips
Dirty White Boys
Down South Boys
Eagle Riders
Eastside Locos
Eastsiders
El Foresteros MC
El Rukens
Familia Stones
Fathers of Anarchy

Florencia 13
Four Corner Hustlers
Gangster Disciples
Grim Reapers MC
Hang Out Boys
Hells Angels MC
Imperial Gangsters
Insane Deuces
Insane Gangsters
Insane Majestics
Insane Popes
Insane Spanish Cobras
Insane Vikings
Iron Horse MC
Juggalos
La Familia
La Raza
Lao Crip
Lao Family Blood
Latin Counts
Latin King
Latin Pachucos
Lomas13
Lomax XIII
Los Chicos
Los Pelones
Lower Riders
Maniac Latin Disciples
Maple Street Goons
MS-13
Matadors MC
Mexican Mafia
Mickey Cobras
Midnight Riders MC
Ñetas
New Breed
Norteños

Northfront Occult

Outlaws MC

P13 Punte

Paisa

Peckerwoods

Players Club Posse

Posse Comitatus

Really Cocky Asshole Killers

Rebel Knights MC

Saints

San Fernando Mexicans

Satan Disciples

Satin Disciples

SHARP

Sioux City Boys

Skinheads

Sons of Freedom MC

Sons of Liberty

Sons of Silence MC

Southside 21

Spanish Cobras

Spanish Disciples Sureño

The Cool Kids

The Fellows

Two Six Nation

United Metro Front

Vagos MC

Vice Lords

Viet Solo Boys

Westside Knights

Westside Locos

Westside Mafia

Westside Mobsters

Westside Villains

Westsiders

White Aryan Resistance

White Boys Only

White Pride X-Club

Young and Wasted

Young Bloods

KANSAS

13 Folks-GDS

357 Crips

4 Corner Hustlers

Bandidos

Bloods

Eastside Locos Sureños

Eastside Vato Locos

El Foresteros MC

Folks

Hoover Crips

Juggalos

Latin Kings

Lawrence Mob

Northsiders

School Yard Crips

Somos Pocos Para Locos

Sons of Silence MC

Sur-13

Traveling Vice Lords

Tru Valley Crips

Vice Lords

Westside Riders

KENTUCKY

Bloods

Crips

Gangster Disciples

Hells Angels MC

Iron Horsemen MC

Latin Kings

MS-13

Outlaws MC

Pagans

Sons of Silence MC

Vice Lords

Wheels of Soul

LOUISIANA

1100 Block Gang

31 Flava's

3-Unit Black-Out Boys

5 Nine Bloods

5-Deuce Crips

5/2 Rock Boys

6th Street Boys

700 Block Gang

7th Ward Hard Heads

800 Block Gang

8th Ward Animals

900 Block Gang

Algiers 1.5

Baby Goonies

Bandidos MC

Bienville Boyz

Blackhawks

Byrd Gang

D-BlockHandy Family

Foucha Gang

Frenchman Money Boys

Gangster Disciples

Garden District Crips

Gray Ghosts

Harvey Hustlers

Jerome Group

Josephine Dog Pound

Lower Third Crips

Maffioso

MS-13

Northside Levin Crips

Northside Posse

Old Mill Quarters Crips

Orange Boy's

Pack of Bastards MC

Prieur & Columbus Boyz

Skull Squad Mafia

Smoke One Click

Sonia Quarter Crips

Sons of Silence MC

Sureños

Tango Blast

Young Cut Boys

Young Gunners

Young Magnolia Melph

MAINE
All Jumpers

Aryan Nation

Crips

Disciples

Exiles

Folk Nation

Fuck Shit Up Gang

Hells Angels MC

Iron Horsemen MC

Latin Kings

L-Town

MS-13

Ñetas

Outlaws MC

P Town Soldiers

Peckerwoods

Saracens

Skinheads

True Somali Bloods

Vice Lords

MARYLAND
18th Street

25 Crew

51 Sandbox

Aryan Brother Hood

Black Guerilla Family

Blitzkrieg MC

Bloods

Crips

Dead Man Incorporated

Folk

Gangster Disciples

Get Money Goons

Go Go Crews

Hells Angels MC

Iron Horsemen MC

Latin Kings

Mara Locos

Mexican Locos

MS-13

Murder Incorporated

Murder Mafia Bloods

New Blood MC

Outlaws MC

Pagan MC

Phantoms MC

Pop Off Mafia

Savage Boys

Street Thug Criminals

Sur-13

Sureños

Thunderguards MC

Trinitarios

Vatos Locos

Warlocks MC

Wheels of Soul MC

Wild Boyz

MASSACHUSETTS
1850 Washington

18th Street

1937 Dorchester Avenue

20 Love

214 Harvard

700 Block

Academy

Academy Homes

Annunciation

Archdale

Aryan Nation Brotherhood

Asian Boyz

Bailey

Barrio Aztecas

Beechland

Bergin Circle Posse

Bicknell

Big Head Boys

Black Gangster Disciples

Black P Stone Nation

Bloods

Bonanno Crime Family

Boylston

Boylston Street

Boyos

Bristol Street Posse

Brunswick / Fayston

Cameron

Carew Block

Castle Square

Castlegate

Cathedral

Cedar Street

Charlame 1

Charlame 2

Cholos

Codman Square	Greenwood Ave	Lowell St Posse
Colombo Crime Family	Greenwood Street	Lucerne St
Colorado / Favre	Grey Rag	Mafilia
Columbia Point	Grupo 25	Mafilia Mass Mobb
Columbia Rd	Grupo 27	Main Street Goons
Crown Path	Gunn Square Posse	Maniac Latin Disciples
Crystal Park Fellaz	H-Block	Mass Ave
Cape Verdean Outlaws	Heath St	Massassoit Street Posse
Dark Side Niggaz	Hells Angels MC	Mexikanemi
Dangerous Little Bloods	Hendry	Mission Hill
DC Crew	Highland	Magnolia
Dominicans Don't Play	Hi-Point	Minoritys Up
Deuce Boys	Hit-Fam	Mongols MC
Diablos	Hizbollah	Morse / Norfolk
Dogg Town Crips	Holworthy	Morse St
Draper	Homes Ave	Mozart
Dudley Street Posse	Hooligans	MS-13
Eastern Ave Posse	Humboldt & Harrishof	Morton St Bricks
Eastern Avenue Boys	Indian Orchard Posse	Mulato Mafia
El Combo que no de deja	Insane Blood Gang	Ñetas
Fairmount Family Plan Farve St.	James Gang MC	New Born Tigers
Five Percenters	Jr Kaos	Norfolk
Forest Hills Pistons	Juggalos	Olney / Norton
Flatbush	Kilby Junior	Orchard Park
Flatbush Posse	Kilby Minor	Orchard St Boyz
Folks	Kilby Original	Orchard Street Bouriquas
Forest Park Gangsters	Kilby Young	Outlaws MC
Franklin Field	Knox St Posse	Outlawz
Franklin Hill	La Familia	Paisa
Franklin Street Posse	La Lowell	Phantom Lords MC
Gangster Disciples	Latin Kings	Road Demons MC
Gangsters	Latin Queens	Rosewood / Thetford
G-Block	Lenox	Ruff Side
Genovese Crime Family	Lenox St	Russian Gangs
G-Mob	Little Tiger	Russian Mob
Greenfield	Long Riders MC	Ruthless For Life MC
Greenwood	Los Solidos	S.W.A.T.

Satans Disciples

Skinheads

Southern Ave

Southside

Southside Posse

Speedwell

Spencer

St James

St Joseph's

Stockton

Sycamore St

Sycamore Street Posse

The Crazy Boys

Tiny Rascal Gangsters

Torrey Street

Vice Lords

Vietnam Vets MC

Villa Victoria

Vine & Forest / Mt Pleasant

Wainwright

Walk Hill

Walnut Pk

Warren Gardens

Wendover

Westville

Wheatland

Wilcock

Wolf Pac

Wood Ave

Woodledge

Woodward

Woolson

Worthington Street Posse

Young Chavos

MICHIGAN

300 Block

Aguitas 16

Avengers MC

Bemis Wealthy Street Boys

Black Gangster Disciple

Black Pistons MC

Brave Heart Ruff Riders

BUG Gang

Campau Cream Team

Cash Ave

Crips

Dallas Neland Alexander

D-Block

Devils Brigade

Devils Disciples MC

Dynasty Gorillas

East Ave

Eastern Worden

Eastside Boys

European Latin Kings

Folks

Forbidden Wheels MC

Gangster Disciples

Good Squad/Full Time Grinders

Grandville Gangsters

Highland's Finest

Highwaymen

Holland Zeeland

Hustle Boys

Insane Unknowns

Ionia Boys

Jefferson Street Gangsters

Jokers MC

Juggalos

Kalamazoo Boys

Kartel of the Streets

La Kilcka

La Raza

Latin Counts

Latin Kings

Leak Boy Mafia

Madison Ave

Maniac Latin Disciples

Mason Street

Mexican Gangster Soldiers

Mexican Mafia

Mexican Mob

New Age Crip

Ñetas

Newman Lane Posse

Nishnob Mob

North North

New World Order

Oakdale Eastern

Outlaws MC

Pine Street

Polo Boyz

Prospect Paper Chasers

Purple Guns

Quimby Boys

Rebels MC

Rikochet Road Knights

Nation Royal Trinity Soldiers

Sheldon Logan

Spanish Cobras

Suicide Locos

Sur-13's

Sureños

Taliban Team

Thug Life

Tres Manos Gangsters

Wanted Thug Brotherhood Nation

Vatos Locos

Vice Lords
Wood street

MINNESOTA
Almighty Vice Lords
Black P Stones
Black Panthers
Brown Pride for Life
Cash Money Boys
Gangster Disciples
Hells Angels MC
Latin Kings
Los Quientes Locas
Mexican Mafia
Native Mob
Native Vice Lords
Norteños 14
Prison Motorcycle Brotherhood
P-Stones
Rough Tough Somalis
Royal Cambodian Bloods
Shotgun Crips
Somali Gangs
Sons of Silence MC
Sureños 13
Texas Syndicate
Vatos Locos
Vice Lords
White Supremacists

MISSISSIPPI
211 Boys
Aryan Brotherhood
Asgards Pistoleros
Bandidos MC
Black Gangster Disciples Bloods
Crips

Gangster Disciples
Galloping Gooses
Handsboro Veterans
Hellified Drama Click
Latin Kings
Mexican Mafia
Simon City Royals
Sons of Silence
Vagos
Vice Lords
Viet Boys

MISSOURI
13 Lennox Wino
10 9 Folks
10 Street Crips
1019 Southside Folks
107 Hoover Crip
10-9 Gangster Disciples
11th Street
124th Athens Park Blood
12th St - Five Ace Deuce
12th Street
12th Street Blood
12th Street Crips
12th Street Disciples
12th Street Hoover Crips
135th Street Piru
13th Street Kcks
16th Street Crew
18th Street King Familia
18th Street Modesto Clique
2 Hard Posse
21st East Bottom Gangsters
21 Hilltop
21 Street Westside
21st Posse Crips

21st Street
21st Street Blood
22nd Street
22nd Street Crips
22nd Street Trey
23rd Street Blood
23rd Street Crips
23rd Street Hard Cores
23rd Street Hustlers
2400 Mob
24th St - Five Ace Deuce
24th Street
24th Street Bloods
24th Street Chelsea Bloods
24th Street Crips
25th Street
25th Street Bloods
25th Street Crips
25th Street Posse Gang
25th Street Quincy Bloods
26th Street Hoover Crips
27 St Belleview Gangsters
2700 Block
2700 Eastside
27th Street
27th Street Bloods
27th Street Crips
27th Street Mob
27th Street Pros
29th Street
29th Street Bloods
29th Street Crips
29th Street Hustlers
29th Street Pros
30's
31st Boys
31st Street

31st Street Crips

31st Street Posse

32nd Street

33rd St K.C. Soldiers

33rd Street

33rd Street Bloods

33rd Street Crips

3400 Woodland

34th Street

35th Street

35th Street Bloods

35th Street Crips

36th Street

36th Street Bloods

36th Street Crips

36th Street Kings

37th Street

38th Street

38th Street Crips

3900 Block

39th Street Midwest Gangsters

39th Street

39th Street Tre-Block

39th Street Bloods

39th Street Crips

39th Street Dogs

39th Street Holy Temple Crips

39th Street Posse

3rd Tre Dog Hustler

3rd Wall Bloods

3rd Wall Crips

3rd World Syndicate

3rd World Players

4 Block 4 Trey

43 Hoover Crips

400 Block Player

40th & Wabash Crips

40th Street

40th Street Crips

41st Street Ghost

42nd Street Crips

4300 Block Insane Gangster

4300 Blood

4300 Brim Side Bloods

4300 Gangsters In Black

43rd 4 Trey Crips

43rd Insane Gangster Crips

43rd St Brooklyn Park Mafia

43rd St

43rd Street Thugs

43rd Street/The Dirty Eastside

44th Street

4500 Bloods

45th

45th Street

45th Street Crips

49th Street

49th Street Bloods

49th Street Dawgs

49th Street Gangster Crips

4th Street Crips

4th Street Guinotte Manor Crip

5 Deuce Brims Bloods

5.2 Eu Crips

50's

50th Crips

5100 Gangsters

51st Bloods

51st Street / 5-Block

51st Street Crips

51st Street Hustlers

5-2 Eastside

52 Pueblo Bloods

52nd Street Gangster Crips

53rd Avalon Gangster Crips

53rd Street

53rd Street Crips

54th Street Blood

54th Street Crips

55th Street Bloods

56th Street Bloods

56th Street Boys

56th Street Crips

56th Street Villains

57 Road Dog Villains

5700 Wc Block Mob

57th Street

57th Street / 5-Block

57th Street Bloods

57th Street Hustler

57th Street Road Dogs

57th Street Rogue Dogs

58th Street / 5-Block

58th Street Hill Dogs

59th Street

59th Street Bloods

59th Street Gangsters

59th Street Hoover Crips

5-Duece Crips

6 Deuce Brims Bloods

60th Blood Hound

60th Street

61st Street

62nd Street

6300 Street

63rd Street Crips

66th Street Blood

67th Street

67th Street Blood

67th Street Crips

68 Mob

6800 Swap Side
68th Street
68th Street Blood
68th Street Crips
68th Street Hustlers
69th Street Bloods
69th Street Crips
69th Street Dawgs
69th Street Niggas
6th Street Crips
7 Duce Crips
7 Miles Blood
7 Oaks Crips
72nd Street Hustlers
73rd Street Crips
74 Folk Crips
74th St Santana Block Crip
74th Street Hoover Crip
75th Street Crips
7th Street Folks
8 Balls
9 Deuce Crips
9-Deuce Bloods
9th Street Dawgs
9th Street Dogs
9th Street Hoover Crips
Ace Block
Aryan Nation
Ashland Park Crips
Asian Boyz
Asian Crips
Asian For Life
Asian Girlz
Athens Park Bloods
Bandits
Banger Squad
Barrio Pobre

Black Gangster Disciples
Black Guerilla Family
Black Mafia Gangster Blood
Blood Game
Blood Lennox
Blood Stone Villains
Bounce Out Boys
Bonner Springs
Blood Border Brothers
Borderland Gang
Bounty Hunter Bloods
Boys From Chihuahua
Broadway Gangsters
Broadway Park Blood
Brown Image Gangsters
Brown Pride Family
Brown Side Locos
Buk
Lao Killers
C-13 Cambridge Crips
Cash Money Boyz
Chain Gang Parolees
Chelsea Bronx
Chelsea Crips
Chestnut Mafia
Circle City Crips
Click Clack Gang
Compton Crips
Corrington Crew
Crazy Ass White Boys
Crimeboyz
Crip Loc Da Gutta Sqaud
Dark Side Posse
Dead Everlasting Gangster
Dead-end Gang
Denver Lane Bloods
Desert Flat Sex Terks

Deuce Blocc
Deuces
Dime Block
Dlb Capone
Double Deuces
Dragon Family
Du Roc Crips
Deuce 4 Gangsters
Deuce 9 Folks
Deuce Deuce Blood
Deuce Deuce Crips
Deuce Lime Brim Bloods
Deuced-Deuce Posse
East Coast Crips
Eastside 15
Eastside Blood
Eastside Click
Eastside Crips
Eastside Folks
Eastside Gangster
Eastside Hathorn Piru Gangster
Eastside Hilltop
Eastside Insane
Eastside Latin Counts
Eastside Locos
Eastside Mexican Locos
Eastside Oceanside Crips
Eastside Posse
Eastside Rollin 20's Crips
Eastside Wet Back Power
Eight Ball Crips
El Foresteros MC
Englewood Family Bloods
Five Ace Deuce
Florencia 13
Fambino's
Familia Chueca

Family Locos

Five Trey Crips

Fog 5100 Original Gangsters

Folks

Freaks

Fremont Hustlers

Frostwood Mob

Galloping Goose MC

Gangster Crips

Gangster Disciples

Gangsters Gear

Gangster Crips

Gracemore Boys

Grape Street Watts Crips

Greenfield Village Posse

Guardian Angels

Guardian Disciples

Hardkore Gangsters

Hells Lovers MC

Hillside Crips

Hillside Hustler

Hillside Mafia

Hilltop

Hilltop Blood

Hoodbound 6700

Hoodsquad

Hoover Crip Gang

107 Hoover Gangster Crips

I'll Rock You Crew

Imperial Gangster Crips

Imperial Valley

Imperial Village

Indian Posse

Indoes Willis Avenue

Inland Empire

Insane Disciples

Insane Family Gangster Blood

Insane Gangster Crips

Insane Gangster Folks

Insane Vato Gangsters

Insane Village Crips

International Gangster Family

Invaders

Jamaican

Jeffrey Manor Gangster Crip

Joplin Honky

Juniper Garden Crips

Knockafella Flame Gang

Kalizion Kansas City Villains

Kingsman Crips

Knocc Out Boyz

Krazy Boyz

La Soul Mafia

La Familia

Langdon Laos Bloods

Laos Boys

Latin Counts

Latin Kings

Latin People

Little Tiny Bitches

Lokitos Gang

Lonely Vets

Lords Of Chaos

Los Madanado

Lynch Mob

Lynwood Mob Bloods

Macken Gangster Crips Malditos

Mexican Disciples

Mexican Boyz

Mexican Kings

Mexican Loco's

Mexican Mafia

Midwest Drifters MC

Money Over Bitches

Money Over Broke Bitches

Moorish Science Temple

MS-13

Mulvthina Loca

Natoma Boyz

Ne Side Blood

700 Block Neighborhood Crips

Neo Nazi

Nes Niggers On Woodland

Nine Nine Mafia Crip

Norteños

North KC Hustlers Crips

North Oak Posse

North Pole Crips

Northeast Side Bloods

Northeast Side Gangsters

Northside Gorilla

Northside Posse

Northwest Evans Park

Norton Block Gangsters Notorious

Nutty Block Crip

O.G.Crips

Original Agnes Gangster

Outlaw Mafia

Pachucos

Parkwood Bloods

Parvin Crew

People 5

People Nation

Pura Familia Loka

Piru Bloods

Playboy Gangsters

Players Club

Pleasure Time

Playboy

Pueblo Bishop

Puma Boys Crips

Quincy Bloods

Quintos In Mexico

Rebels 13

Raymond Street Hustlers

Rearview Players Crips

Red Mob Gangsters

Riverside Posse Crips

Rogue Dog Villains

Rollin 20's Crips

Rollin 30's Crips

Rollin 40's Crips

Rollin 60's Blood

Rollin 60's Crips

Rollin 80's Bloods

Ready To Kill

Ruskin Way Boys

Saddle Tramps

Saint Disciples

Saint Margaret

Samoan Satans

Spanish Disciples

Scarface School Yard Crips

Six Eight Gang

Southeast Pachucos

Seven Deuce Lime Street Bloods

Shotgun Crips

Six Deep Crips

Six Duce Crips

Six Deuce Brim

Six Tra

Six-Deuce Bloods

Sk7 Skaters

Skinheads

Somali Gangs

Sons Of Samoa

Southside 13

Southside 60's

Southside Crips

Southside Family Bloods

Southside Posse

Southside Villains

Spanish Disciple

Spanish Gangsters

Sur Por Vida

Sur-13

Sureños

Swampside Taggers

Tas-Dog Crips

Taliban Gang

Terrace Lake Crips

Tra Dog Crips

Tra Side Gangster

Tra-9

Tra-Side

Traside Mobb

Tre Wall Tre-Tre

Tre Block 33

Tre-9

Tre-Deuce Gangster Crips

Tree Top Piru

Tre Side Gangsters

Tra-Side Gorillas

Twampside/1/4 Block

Underground Crips

Uptown Players

Vagos Trece

Vagos MC

Vatos Loco

V-Boys

Varrio Delinquentes

Viet For Life

Vice Lords

Vietnamese Crips

Village Boyz Bloods

Waldo Crip

Westbluff Blood

Western Bloods

Westside 111 Crips

Westside 18 Malandros

Westside 23 Holly Block Gang

Westside 41st Crip

Westside Bloods

Westside Chronicles Blood

Westside El Centro

Westside Hoover Crips

Westside Latin Counts

Westside Locos

Westside Pride Family Loco

Westside Player

Westside Rollin 40's

Westside Rolling 60's

Westside Traviesos

Wheels Of Soul MC

Wiggers

Woodland Crips

Young Oriental Gangsters

MONTANA

406 Dedicated Family

Aryan Circle of Texas

Bandidos MC

Bandits

Bloods

Cossacs

Crips

Dirty White Boys

Galloping Goose MC

Gangster City Family

Gangster Disciples

Hombres

Insane Vice Lords

Juggalo
Latin Kings
Modern
Modern Outlaws
Mongols MC
National Socialist Skinheads
Norteños
Outlaws MC
Peckerwoods
Pride Member Bandidos
Soldier of Seven
Suicide Mafia
Supreme White Power
Sureños
Texas Dirty White Boys
White Supremacist

NEBRASKA
18th Street
AM Vets
Bandidos MC
Crips
Eastside Loco 13
Eastside Locos
Gangster Disciples
Goon Squad
Hells Angels
Latin Kings
Lomas
MS-13
MSR137
Must Be Criminal
Norteños
Rebels 13
South Family Bloods
Southside 13
Southside Winos

Sureños
Under Age Kriminal

NEVADA
28th Street
Bandidos
Barrio Naked City
Lil Lokes
Mongols
Nevada Trece
Norteños
San Chucos
Sureños
Skinheads
Vagos

NEW HAMPSHIRE
Bay State Skinheads
Bloods
Brothers of the White Warriors
Chinese Mafia
Combatants
Crips
Diamond Kings
Dominions
Folk
Gangster Disciples
Hells Angels MC
Iron Eagles MC
Juggalos
Kaotic Kings of Destruction
Latin Gangster Disciples
Latin Kings
Milford & Company
Mountain Men MC
MS-13
Outlaws MC

Pagans MC
Red Villain Gangstas
Rough Riders
Sureños
Trinitarios

NEW JERSEY
135 Piru
464Piru
793 Bloods
Brick City Brims
Haitian Outlaws
Hoover Crips
Grape Street Crips
G-Shine Bloods
Hells Angels MC
Latin Kings
MS-13
Ñetas
Pagans
Trinitarios
Sex Money Murder

NEW MEXICO
Bandidos
Eastside
Juggalos
Los Padillas Gang
MS-13
San Jose Gang
Southside Loco
Sureños
Thugs Causing Kaos
Vagos
Westside
Westside Locos

NEW YORK

18th Street
Aryan Brotherhood
Bishops
Black Gangster Disciple
Black Panther
Bloods
Crips
El Grupo 27
Haitian Mafia
Hells Angels MC
Juggalos
Latin Kings
Mexikanemi
MS-13
Ñetas
Outlaws
Pagans MC
Paisa
Peoples Nation
Raza Unida
Skinheads
Sureños
Texas Syndicate
Thug Out Players
Trinitarios
Vagos
Vatos Locos
Warlocks MC
Wheels of Soul MC

NORTH CAROLINA

13 Meadow Wood Memphis Bloods
18th Street
174 Valentine Bloods
20's Neighborhood Piru
21st Crips

318 Crips
4-Trey Gangster Crips
5 Deuce Hoover Crips
5 Line Eastside Bounty Hunters
8 Trey Crips
9 Tek
9 Trey
9 Trey Gangsters
910 MOB
A Squad
Aryan Brotherhood
Aryan Nation
Ashboro St Bloods
Ashton Forrest Bloods
Asian Boyz
Avalon Gangster Crips
B St Bloods
Beaver Creek South
BL-50 Bloods
Black Gangster Disciples
Black Guerilla Family
Black P Stones
Bonnie Doone Folk
Bounty Hunter Assassins
Bounty Hunter Bloods
Bounty Hunter Villains
Brown Pride
Brown Pride Aztecs
Bunce Road Bloods
Cambridge Arms Bloods
Conservative Vice Lords
D-Block Bloods
DC Bounty Hunters
Dead Man Incorporated
Desperados MC
Deuce 13
Eastside MOB Piru

Eastside Murder Boyz
Eight Trey Crips
Fairlane Acres Crips
Five Percenters
Flame Squad
Folk Nation
Foxfire Bloods
Fruit Town Brims
Gangster Disciples
Get Money Clique
Ghost Gangster Disciples
Gangster Killer Bloods
Grape Street Crips
Graveyard Crips
Hells Angels MC
Hoover 107 Crips
HTO Bloods
IGC 973
Insane Gangster Crips
Insane Gangster Disciples
Jbirds
Juggalos
Kings/Dons
Latin Kings
Loch Boys
Major Grind
Mafia Malditos
Mexican Mafia
Misplaced Souls MC
Money Over Bitches Bloods
Money Money
Hungry Soldiers
Money Maker Squad
MS-13
Murch Mob
Murder Bloods
Nazi Low Riders

Ñetas

New Jersey Mafia

Norte-14

Norteños

NWA Bloods

Outlaws MC

People Nation

P-NOX

Queensmore Bloods

Real Street Niggas

Red Devils MC

Rollin 20's Crips

Rollin 30's Crips

Rollin 40's Crips

Rollin 60's Crips

Savoy Heights Posse

Seabrook Bloods

Sex Shaw Road Crips

South Central 81st Crips

Sur-13

Tiny Rascals Gang

Trap Squad

United Blood Nation

Valentine's Day

Vatos Locos

Westside MOB Piru

Westside Piru

NORTH DAKOTA
Folk Nation

Gangster Disciples

Native Mob Crips & Bloods

Sons of Silence

OHIO
1300 Area Rap Gang

187 Boys

33rd Street

4-Block

52/52 Niggas

600 Block/Hill Top Gangsters

614 Boy Foundation

22nd Piru Bloods

9 Kings

A.C. 357

Akron Larceny Boys

Ak-Town / 330/ 440 / 216

All About Money

Aryan Brotherhood

Aryan Nation

Asian Crips

Avengers MC

Ayers Street Playas

Baller Boy Mafia

Banished Brothers MC

Black Pistons MC

Bloodline

Bottom Hawks

Brick Boys

Brothers MC

Brother's of the Hammer MC

Buckeye Folks

Chest Block Gangsters

Chestola

Da Kennel

Dayton View Hustlers

D-Block/21st Street Killers

Dem Block Boys

Derelects MC

Diamond Cut

Diamond Dogs MC

Dirt and Grime MC

Dirty South

Down the Way

Down Town Area Rap Gang

Eastside Bloods

Eastside Connection

Folks Gangster Afficial

Gangster Disciple Folks

Gangster Disciples

Gangster Killer Bloods

Get Money Boys

Get Money Goonies

Goonies

Greenwich Village Crew

G-Unit Crips

Hammerskins

Head Bustin Niggas

Heartless Felonies

Heightz Boyz

Hells Angels MC

Hilltop 7714 Crips

Hough Heights Boys/Hough

Harlem Boys

Hunnid Block Gang

Iceberg Bloods

Johnston Block

Kaika Klan Outlaws

King Cobra Boys

Kinsman County/Rollin 40 Crips

K-Town Gangsters

Laffer Block

Laird Block Gangsters

Lake Boys

Lakeshore Boys

Laotian Crips

Latin Kings

Lovers Lane Crips

Laclede Parkview Ave

Madison Madhouse

Middle Avenue Zone

Money Go Gettas
Money Over Bitches
MS-13
New Northside Gangsters
Niggas From Laffer
North Coast MC
North Coast XII MC
Northside Gangstas
Original Killers
Otterbien Blood Mafia
Outlaws MC
Quinn Street Crew
Pagans MC
Rated R
Renegades MC
Rollin 20 Crips
S1W Southwest
Satans MC
Sherwood Ave
Shorb Block
Shorb Block Hustlers
Sin City Disciples MC
Skinheads Against Racial Prejudice
Skinheads Skulls
Soup City Boys
South Block Gangsters
Southwest Akron Thugs
Southwest Boyz
Southwest Gangsters
Southside Gangsters
StarBoyz
Stay Focus Rap Gang
Strays MC
Suffocated Records
Sureños 13
The Breed MC
The Brother's MC

The Circle
The Notch Boys
The Team /The Squad
The Unit
Tribe
Up the Way
Valley Boys
Valley Niggas On Top
Valley-Lo
Vice Lords
Wages
Wheels of Soul MC
White Supremacists
Young Blooded Thugs
Young Kaika Boys
Young Kaika Girls
Young Kelly Boys
Young Street Goonies
Zone 3 Bloods
Zone 7
Zone 8
Zulus MC

OKLAHOMA
Asian Gang
Bandidos MC
Bloods
Border Brothers
Crips
Hoovers
Indian Brotherhood
Juggalos
Mongols MC
MS-13
Native American Gang
Nazi Low Riders
Norteño

Mexican Mafia
Outlaws MC
Sur Trece
Carnales
Sureños
Unidos en Uno
Universal Aryan Brotherhood
USO Family

OREGON
18th Street
Brother Speed
Brown Pride
Columbia Villa Crips
Gangster Disciples
Hmong Pride
Hoover Criminal
Kerby Blocc Crips
Lincoln Park Bloods
Masters of Destruction
MS-13
Mongols MC
Norteños
Rolling 60's Crips
Southside Trece
Unthank Park Hustler
Vagos MC
West Coast Mafia Crip
Westside Mob Crips
Woodlawn Park Bloods

PENNSYLVANIA
18th Street
AC Skins
Aryan Brotherhood
Aryan Circle
Aryan Resistance Militia

Asian Boyz
Barbarians MC
Barrios Aztecas
Black Gangster Disciples
Black Guerilla Family
Black Jack MC
Bloods
Border Brothers
Breed Brick Yard Mafia
DC Crews
Dirty White Boys
G-27
Gangster Disciples
Green Dragons
Hells Angels
HPL Il Morte
Insane Gangster Disciple
Insane Unknowns
Juggalos
Kensington 215
Keystone United
Latin Kings
Low Crips
Mavericks
Mexican Mafia
Mexikanemi
MS-13
Nazi Low Riders
Neo Nazi
Ñetas
New Mexico Syndicate
Norteños
Nuestra Familia
Outlaws MC
Pagans MC
Paisa
Raza Unida

Sin City Disciples MC
Skinheads
Soldiers of Aryan Culture
Street Familia
StrongArm Production
Mexican Mafia
Sureño 13
Sureños
Tangos
Tango Blast
Texas Chicano Brotherhood
Texas Family
Texas Syndicate
Tribe MC
Trinitarios
Vagos
Vice Lords
Wardogs MC
Warlocks MC
Warrior Society
Wheels of Soul MC

PUERTO RICO
Borinquen Street Gang
Brisas De Salinas
Grupo 25
Grupo 27
La Marina
La Montaña Public Housing
Latin Kings
Los Ñetas
Los 31
Los 25
Nuevo Grupo 25
ONU Rompe
San Andres Public Housing

RHODE ISLAND
18 Street
Black Gangster Disciples
Clown Town Crip
Darkside Rascals
Hanover Boyz
Hells Angels MC
Latin Kings
Laos Pride
MS-13
Ñetas
Oriental Rascals
Original Bloods
Original Crip Gang
Providence Street Boyz
South Street Boys
Sur-13
Vagos MC
Young Bloods

SOUTH CAROLINA
031 Piru
1212
10 Mile Boys
18th Street
3rd Pound
3VL
4-4
4 Mile Boys
41 Boys
48 Boys
4G
5 Percenters
58Tres
6 Mile Boys
8 Trey Crips

9 Tre Boys
9th Ward
Adams Run Bottom Boyz
Band of Brothers MC
Bedroc
Black Gangster Disciples
Black Mafia Black "P" Stone
Bloods-031
Bloods MC
Boogie Woogie
Bounty Hunters
Church Hill Boyz
Converse Street Gang
County Boys
Creekside Crips
Cross Cut
Cross The Track
Dem Country Bois
Devils Rejects
Down the Island
Duncan Park Gang
East West Forest/Forest Boys
Eastside
Eastside Crips
Eastside Folk
Farside/West Cash
Ferry Ferry
Folk Nation
G Shine
Gangster Killer Bloods
Gangster Disciples
Gatas Petersfield Jungle Boyz
Geddy's Ville Boyz
Greenview Thugs
Hells Angels MC
Hilltop-Crips
Hoover Crips

Insane Gangster Disciples
Johns Island Bloods
Kampa Bois
Kampa Style Villa Posse
Kings Court
Laos Crips and Bloods
Latin Kings
Lemon Tree Bois
Misguided Brotherhood
MS-13
Natural Born Assassins
New Black Panthers
Neighborhood Bloods
Norte 14
Northside Bloods
Northside Gang
OB Orleans Garden Boys
Outlaws MC
Paisas
Park Hill Gang
Parkers Pine Hurst Posse
Pineland Slap Boyz
Red Devils MC
Rivaside Goons
Rollin 20's
Rollin 90 Crips
Souf Santee
Sosik Clik
Southside
Southside 3rd Ward
Straight Shooters MC
Sur-13
Sureños
SWAMP
Texas Community Gangsta
The Doolie Hill Gang
The Sand Hill Gang

The Ville Thunderguards
Tibwin Bois
Trap Star Soldiers
Tree Top Piru
Town Gorillas
Trey 9 Bloods
Tville Bloods
UpTop Soldiers
Urban Warriors
Vatos Locos
Warhorse Brotherhood
Warlocks MC
Westside
Westside Bloods
Wild Bunch

SOUTH DAKOTA
Bandidos
Conservative Vice Lords
Darkside Family
East River Skins
East River Souls
Eastside Thugs
Gangster Disciples
Main Street Crips
Native Latin Kings
Nomadz
Northside Gangster Disciples
Red Iron Players
Sur-13
The Boyz
Thug Line
Tre Tre Gangster Crips
True Villain Bloodz
Vagos
Warlords
West Mafia Crip Family
Westside Piru Bloodz

TENNESSEE

103 Watts Varrio Grape Street Crips
107 Hoover Crips
Five Percenters
52 Hoover Crips
Aryan Brotherhood
Aryan Circle
Aryan Nation
Asian Pride
Athens Park Bloods
Boone Height Mafia Crips
Bounty Hunter Bloods
Brotherhood Forever
Brown Pride
Confederate Sons MC
Crazy White Boys
E87 Kitchen Crips
Gangster Disciples
Ghost Vice Lords
Imperial Insane Vice Lords
Juggalos
Kempo Drive Posse
Kurdish Pride
Latin Kings
Memphis Mob
Mexican Mafia
MS-13
Outlaws MC
Prison Motorcycle Brotherhood
Renegades MC
Rollin 60's Crips
Skyline Piru
Sureños
Sureños 13
Tiny Rascal Gangsters
Traveling Vice Lords
TreeTop Piru

Unknown Vice Lords
Vice Lords
White Aryan Resistance
Woodlawn Crips

TEXAS

Aryan Brotherhood
Aryan Brotherhood of Texas
Aryan Circle
Asian Pride
Bandidos MC
Barrio Azteca
Barrio Azteca Sureños
Black Gangster Disciples
Bloods
Brown Pride
Cliques
Combes Crazy Clique
Crips
Cuchillos
Drop City Thugz
Eastside Homeboys
Eastside Locos
Eastside Pharr
Fair Park
Ghetto Starz
Hermanos Pistoleros Latinos
Highland Hills Posse
Ironriders MC
Kings Loco 8 Bandidos
Krazy Jokers
Las Palmas Indios
Latin Kings
Loco 13
Los Compadres MC
Los Homeboys
Mexican Mafia

Mexikanemi
MS-13
NOR 14
Norteños
North Dallas Vagos
Northside Locos
Notorious Thugs
Orejons Partido Revolucionario Mexicanos
Pharrolitos
Pleasant Grove Vatos
Po'Boys
PRM Valluco
Puro Tango Blast
Raza Unida
Southside Bandidos
Southside Donna
Southside EVW
Southside Folk
Sur-13
Sureño 13
Tango Blast
Texas Chicano Brotherhood
Texas Mafia
Texas Mexican Mafia
Texas Syndicate
Tongo Westside
Tri-City-Bombers
Vagos MC
Vallucos
Varrio Northside
Varrio Northside Vato Locos
West Texas Tangos
Westside Aquas Harlingen
Westside Bowie Town A's
Westside Filmore A's
Westside Los Vecinos
White Knights

UTAH

Asian Boyz
Baby Regulators
Bandidos MC
Barons
Black Mafia Gangsters
Brother Speed
Crown Latin Kings
Fourth Reich
Iraqi Taliban
Kerberos
King Mafia Disciples
Mongols MC
MS-13
Murder One Family
Norteños
Oriental Boy Soldiers
Oriental Laotian Gangsters
Samoans in Action
Silent Aryan Warriors
Soldiers of the Aryan Culture
Sons of Samoa
Sons of Silence MC
Sundowners
Tiny Oriental Posse
Tongan Crip Gangsters
Vagos MC
Sudanese Gangs
Sureños
Varrio Loco Town
Vice Lords

VERMONT

No reporting

VIRGINIA

18th Street Gang
36th Street Bang Squad
43/Hollywood Church Boyz
43 MOB
44 MOB
52 Hoover Crips
9 Trey Bloods
9 Trey Gangsters
Aryan Brotherhood
Asian Dragon Family
Bang Squad
Black Gangster Disciples
Black P Stone Nation
Black Pistons MC
Blackout Bloods
Bloods
Bounty Hunter Bloods
Brown Pride
Camp Grove Killas
Ching-A-Lings MC
Cross Roads Crew
Culmore City
Cypress Manor Posse Crips
Cypress Manor Posse Bloods
Devils Grip
Dragon Family
Dump Squad
Fifth Ward
Five Percenters
Florencia 13
Folk Nation
Freeney Boyz
Gangster Killer Bloods
Gangster Disciples
Ghost Riders MC
Hells Angels MC

Hill Street
Hoffler Boyz
Holiday Death Chamber
Holiday Death Crew
Hot Boyz
Illusions MC
Insane Gangster Disciples
Iron Coffins MC
Kings of Richmond County
La Primera
La Privada Riderz
Lake Kennedy Posse Bloods
Latin Homies
Latin Kings
La Clique Original
MS-13
Marauders MC
Merciless Souls
Mexican Mafia
Mexican Pride
Mongols MC
MS-13
Murk Squad
Nine Trey Gangsta
Nomads MC
Norteños 14
OO6 Blitz
Outlaws MC
Pagans MC
People Nation
Piru Pound Property
Renegades MC
Road Dragons
Rolling 90's
San Diego Eastside Piru
Scorpions MC
Shoot-em Up Boys

South Suffolk Gangsters Crips
Southside/202 SQUAD
Southside Locos
Sureños
Stack Squad
Sur-13
The Good Ones
Titans MC
Tradesmen MC
Tiny Rascal Gangsters
Tribe MC
Tucker Hill
Unknown Fools
Valentines Bloods
Vice Lords
Virginia Raiders MC
Warlocks MC
Warlords
Zetas

WASHINGTON
18th Street
74 Hoover Criminals
74 Hoover Crips
Aryan Brotherhood
Aryan Family
Bandidos MC
Black Gangster Disciples
Big Dog Norteños
Black Guerilla Family
Chinese Triads
Deuce 8 Black Gangster Disciples
Deuce 8 Gangster Disciples
Deuce-0's
Deuce-9's
Down With the Crew Gangster Disciples

Drama Boyz
East African Gangs
European Kindred
Florencia 13
Green Rags
Hakenkreuz
Hells Angels MC
Hilltop
Holly Park Crips
Hoover Crips
Juggalos
Kitchen Crips
La Fuma Bloods
Lakewood Hustler Crips
Latin Kings
Lil Valley Lokos 13
Lil Valley Lokotes 13
Low Profile Gangsters
Little Valley Locotos
Magic Wheels
MS-13
Mexican Mafia
Mongols
Native Son Bloods
Nine Street Crips
Norteños
Northwest Boot Boys
Oriental Boyz
Oriental Fantasy Boys
Outlaws MC
Paisas
Peckerwoods
Playboy Gangster
Playboys 13
Rancho San Pedro 3rd Street Skinheads
Somali Gangs

Sons of Samoa
South Asian Gangs
South Asian Gangsters
Southside Tokers
Street Mobb
Sur-13
Sureños
Tiny Rascal Gangsters
Union Street Black Gangster Disciples
Varrio Campo Vida
Varrio Locos 13
Vatos Locos
Yesler Terrace Bloods
Young Oriental Troop
Young Seattle Boys

WEST VIRGINIA
Black Guerilla Family
Junk Yard Dogs
Latin Kings
Pagans MC
Warlocks MC

WISCONSIN
10th St Gangster Disciples
12th St Gangster Disciples
16 Gun Clique
2-1's
25 Vice Lords
26 Vice Lords
29 Hard Heads
6th St Gangster Disciples
Big O Ones
Black Cobras MC
Black Gangster Disciples
Black Mob

Black P Stones

Black Pistons MC

Block 25th

Brothers Of The Struggle

Brown Pride 13

Burleigh Zoo

Chicago Gangster Disciples

Chicago Vice Lords

City Of Clybourne

Clanton 13

Conservative Vice Lords

Dirty South Gangster Disciples

Dukes 13

Eastside Gangsters

Eastside Mafiosos

Everybody Knows

El Rukins

Four Corner Hustler

Gangster Disciples

Gangster Pimpin

Getto Boys

Hot Boys

Imperial Gangsters

Imperial Gangster Disciples

Insane Unknowns

Insane VL

La Familia

Latin Bloods

Latin Kings

Los Primos

Los Veteranos 13

Maniac Latin Disciples

Maple Street

Mexican Posse 13

Mexican Sureños Locos Ochos

Midtown Gangster Disciples

Murda Mobb

Nash Street Boys

Native Mob

Northside Gangster Disciples

Orchestra Alanis

Outlaws MC

Players

Sons Of Loyalty

Sovereign Nation Warriors

Spanish Cobras

Spanish Gangster Disciples

Sureños 13

The 4's

The Loonies

Tiny Locos 13

Traveling Vice Lords

Tre Eights

Vice Lords

Wild 100's

WYOMING

307 Southside

Bandidos

Bloods

Brown Pride

Gangster Disciples

Juggalos

Kriniminals Sureños

Lincoln Park

Southside Locos

Sur-13

Wreck Team

APPENDIX B. MDTOs Alliances and Rivals

CARTEL	ALIGNED WITH	RIVALS
The Sinaloa Cartel (aka Guzman-Loera Organization or Pacific Cartel)	Hermanos de Pistoleros Latinos New Mexico Syndicate Los Carnales Latin Kings Mexican Mafia (California) Sureños MS-13 Arizona Mexican Mafia (Old & New) Wet Back Power Sinaloa Cowboys West Texas Tangos Los Negros Valencia Cartel (Considered a branch of the Sinaloa Cartel) Sonora Cartel (Considered a branch of the Sinaloa Cartel) Colima Cartel (Considered a branch of the Sinaloa Cartel) Border Brothers (California) Border Brothers (Arizona)	Los Zetas Cardenas-Guillen Cartel (Gulf) Tijuana Cartel Beltran-Leyva Cartel Juarez Cartel
La Familia Michoacana Cartel (Formerly part of Los Zetas under the authority of the Gulf Cartel)	Sinaloa Cartel Cardenas-Guillen Cartel (Gulf) Surenos MS-13 West Texas Tangos	Los Zetas Cardenas-Guillen Cartel (Gulf Cartel) The Beltran-Leyva Cartel Vincente Carrillo-Fuentes Cartel (Juarez Cartel)
Los Zetas	Vincente Carrillo-Fuentes Cartel (Juarez) Beltran-Leyva Cartel Barrio Azteca Hermanos de Pistoleros Latinos Mexikanemi Texas Syndicate MS-13	Arellano-Felix Cartel (Tijuana) Cartel de la Sierra (Sierra Cartel) Sinaloa Cartel La Familia Michoacana Cartel Cardenas-Guillen Cartel (Gulf)

CARTEL	ALIGNED WITH	RIVALS
Cardenas-Guillen Cartel (Gulf Cartel)	Sinaloa Cartel La Familia Michoacana Cartel Hermanos de Pistoleros Latinos Partido Revolutionary Mexicano Raza Unida Texas Chicano Brotherhood	Los Zetas La Familia Michoacana Cartel The Sinaloa Cartel
Vincente Carrillo-Fuentes Cartel (Juarez Cartel)	Los Zetas Hermanos de Pistoleros Latinos Barrio Azteca New Mexico Syndicate Los Carnales	The Sinaloa Cartel La Familia Michoacana Cartel
The Beltran-Leyva Cartel (expected to soon be taken over by the Sierra Cartel)	Los Zetas	Los Zetas La Familia Michoacana Cartel
Arellano-Felix Cartel (Tijuana Cartel)	Mexican Mafia (California) Sureños Arizona Mexican Mafia (Old & New) Border Brothers (California)	Los Zetas The Sinaloa Cartel

APPENDIX C. Federal Gang Task Forces

FBI SAFE STREETS GANG TASK FORCES

Alabama

Mobile Violent Crime Joint Task Force

Northeast Alabama Safe Streets Task Force

Alaska

Anchorage Safe Street Task Force

Arizona

Northern Arizona Violent Gang Task Force

Southwest Arizona Safe Streets Task Force

Violent Street Gang Task Force

Arkansas

Metro Gang-Joint Task Force

California

Central Coast Safe Streets Violent Gang Task Force

Central Valley Gang Impact Team Task Force

East County Regional Gang Task Force

Gang Impact Team (Riverside)

Imperial Valley Safe Streets Task Force

Kern County Violent Crime/Gang Task Force

Los Angeles Metro Task Force On Violent Gangs

North Bay Regional Gang Task Force

North Central Coast Gang Task Force

North County Regional Gang Task Force

Sacramento Valley Gang Suppression Team

Safe Streets East Bay Task Force

San Francisco Safe Streets Violent Crimes Task Force

San Gabriel Valley Safe Streets Violent Gang Task Force

Santa Ana Gang Task Force

Santa Clara County Violent Gang Task Force

Solano County Violent Gang Safe Streets Task Force

South LA County Violent Crimes Task Force

Stockton Violent Crime Task Force

Ventura County RIACT

Violent Crime Task Force-Gang Group

Colorado

Denver Metro Gang Safe Streets Task Force

Southern Colorado Violent Gang Safe Streets Task Force

Connecticut

Bridgeport Safe Streets Gang Violent Crimes Task Force

New Haven Safe Streets Task Force

Northern Connecticut Violent Crimes Gang Task Force

Delaware

Delaware Violent Crime Safe Streets Gang Task Force

Florida

Daytona Beach Safe Streets Task Force

Jacksonville Criminal Enterprise Investigative Task Force

Metro Orlando Safe Streets Gang Task Force

Palm Beach County Gang and Criminal Organization Task Force

South FL. Gang/Criminal Organization Task Force

Tampa Bay Safe Streets Task Force

Georgia

Atlanta Criminal Enterprise Task Force

Central Savannah River Area Safe Streets Gang Task Force

Conasauga Major Offenders Task Force

Hall County Major Offenders Task Force

Northwest Georgia Criminal Enterprise Task Force

Southwest Georgia Gang Task Force

Idaho

Treasure Valley Metro Gang Task Force

Illinois

Eastern Illinois Safe Streets Task Force

Joint Task Force on Gangs – Tactical

Joint Task Force on Gangs - West

Joint Task Force on Gangs II

Joint Task Force on Gangs-1

Metro East Safe Streets

North Suburban Gang Task Force

Peoria Area Safe Streets Task Force

Quad Cities Fed Gang Task Force

Will County Violent Crimes Task Force

Indiana

Eastern Central Indiana Safe Streets Task Force

Fort Wayne Safe Streets Gang Task Force

Gary Response Investigative Team

Gang Response Investigative Team Tippecanoe

Indianapolis Metro Gang Safe Streets Task Force

Wabash Valley Safe Streets Task Force

Iowa

Cedar Rapids Safe Streets Task Force

Kentucky

Northern Kentucky Safe Streets Task Force

Louisiana

Calcasieu Parish Gang Task Force

Capital Area Gang Task Force

Central Louisiana Gang Task Force

New Orleans Gang Task Force

Northeast Louisiana Gang Task Force

Shreveport Task Force

South Central Louisiana Safe Streets Task Force

Maine

Southern Maine Gang Task Force

Maryland

Prince George's County Safe Streets Task Force

Violent Crime Safe Streets Initiative

Massachusetts

North Shore Gang Task Force

Southeastern Massachusetts Gang Task Force

Western Massachusetts Gang Task Force

Michigan

Benton Harbor Violent Crime Task Force

Detroit Violent Gang Task Force

Genesee County Safe Streets Task Force

Mid-Michigan Safe Streets Task Force

Oakland County Safe Streets Task Force

Minnesota

Twin Cities Safe Streets Violent Gang Task Force

Mississippi

Jackson Safe Streets Task Force

Southeast Mississippi Safe Streets Task Force

Missouri

Kansas City Metropolitan Gang Task Force

St. Louis Safe Streets Gang Task Force

Montana

Big Sky Safe Streets Task Force

Central Montana Gang Task Force

Nebraska

Central Nebraska Drug and Safe Streets Task Force

Greater Omaha Safe Streets Task Force

Nevada

Las Vegas Safe Streets Gang Task Force

New Hampshire

New Hampshire Safe Streets Task Force

New Jersey

Jersey Shore Gang and Criminal Organization Task Force

South Jersey Violent Incident/Gang Task Force

South Jersey Violent Offender and Gang Task Force

Violent Crime Criminal Enterprise Task Force

Violent Crimes Incident Task Force

New Mexico

Albuquerque Safe Streets HIDTA Gang Task Force

Four Corners Safe Streets Task Force

Southern New Mexico Street Gang Task Force

New York

Buffalo Safe Streets Task Force

Capital District Gang Task Force

Hudson Valley Safe Streets Violent Gang Task Force

Long Island Gang Task Force

Westchester County Violent Crimes Task Force

North Carolina

Charlotte Safe Streets Task Force

Piedmont Triad Safe Streets Gang Task Force

Raleigh Durham Safe Streets Task Force

Wilmington Safe Streets Task Force

Ohio

Greater Akron Area Safe Streets Task Force

Mahoning Valley Violent Crime Task Force

Miami Valley Safe Streets Task Force

Stark County, Ohio Violent Crime/Fugitive Task Force

Oklahoma

Oklahoma City Metropolitan Gang Task Force

Oregon

Portland Metro Gang Task Force

Pennsylvania

Bucks County Violent Gang Task Force

Capital Cities Safe Streets Task Force

Delaware Valley Violent Crimes Task Force

Erie Area Gang Law Enforcement Task Force

Greater Pittsburgh Safe Streets Task Force

Lehigh Valley Violent Crimes Task Force

Philadelphia Violent Gang Task Force

Safe Streets Violent Crimes Task Force

Safe Streets Violent Drug Gang Task Force

Steamtown Gang Task Force

SW Pennsylvania Safe Streets Task Force .

Puerto Rico

Aguadilla Regional Enforcement Team

Fajardo Regional Enforcement Team

Ponce Safe Streets Task Force

Safe Streets Task Force

Rhode Island

Rhode Island Violent Crimes/Gang Task Force

South Carolina

Columbia Violent Gang Task Force

Pee Dee Violent Crime Task Force

Tennessee

Chattanooga Safe Streets Task Force

Knoxville Headquarters Safe Streets Violent Crimes Task Force

Nashville Violent Crimes Gang Task Force

Safe Streets Task Force HQ City

Texas

Austin Violent Crime Gang/Organized Crime Task Force

Corpus Christi Violent Crimes Task Force

East Texas Area Gang Initiative

El Paso Street and Prison Gang Task Force

Houston Coastal Safe Streets Task Force

Multi-Agency Gang Task Force

Rio Grand Valley Violent Crimes Task Force

San Antonio Safe Streets Violent Crimes Task Force

Southeast Texas Safe Streets Task Force

Tarrant County Safe Streets Task Force

Violent Crimes and Major Offenders and Gang Task Force

West Texas Anti-Gang Team

West Texas Area Major Offender Task Force

Utah

Northern Utah Criminal Apprehension Team

Safe Streets Violent Crime Task Force

Virginia

Richmond Area Violent Enterprise Task Force

South Piedmont Virginia Gang Task Force

The Peninsula Safe Streets Task Force

Tidewater Violent Crimes Task Force

Washington

Seattle Safe Streets and Gang Task Force

South Sound Gang Task Force

Southwest Washington Safe Streets Task Force

Spokane Violent Crime Gang Enforcement Team

Tri-Cities Violent Crime Gang Enforcement Team

Washington, D.C.

WFO/MPD/Safe Streets Gang Task Force

West Virginia

Eastern Panhandle and Potomac Highlands Safe Streets Task Force

Huntington Violent Crimes/Drug Task Force

Wisconsin

Gang-Rock County Task Force

Greater Racine Gang Task Force

ATF VIOLENT CRIME IMPACT TEAMS (VCIT)

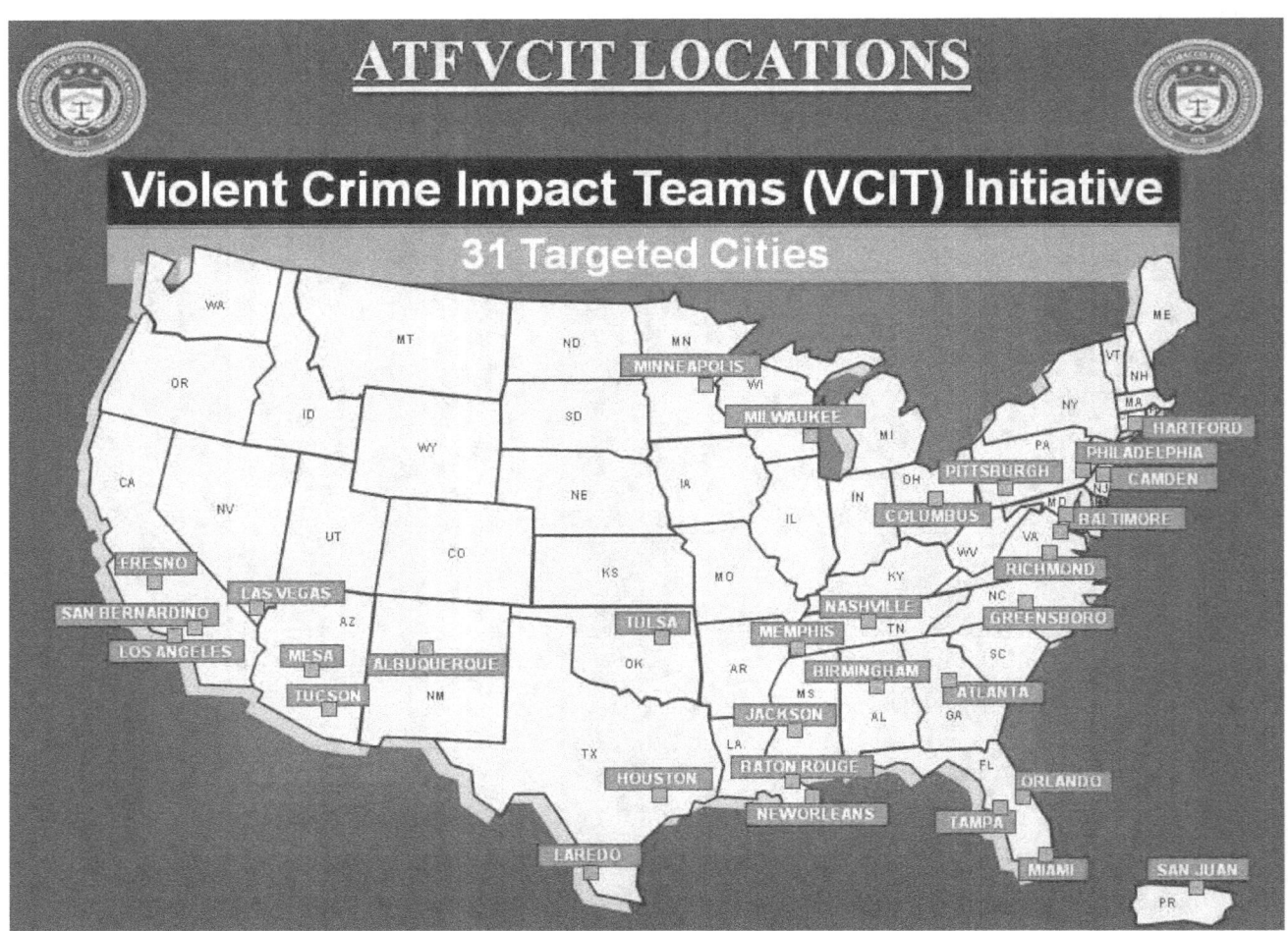

Source: ATF

ICE OPERATION COMMUNITY SHIELD (OCS) INITIATIVE TARGETS

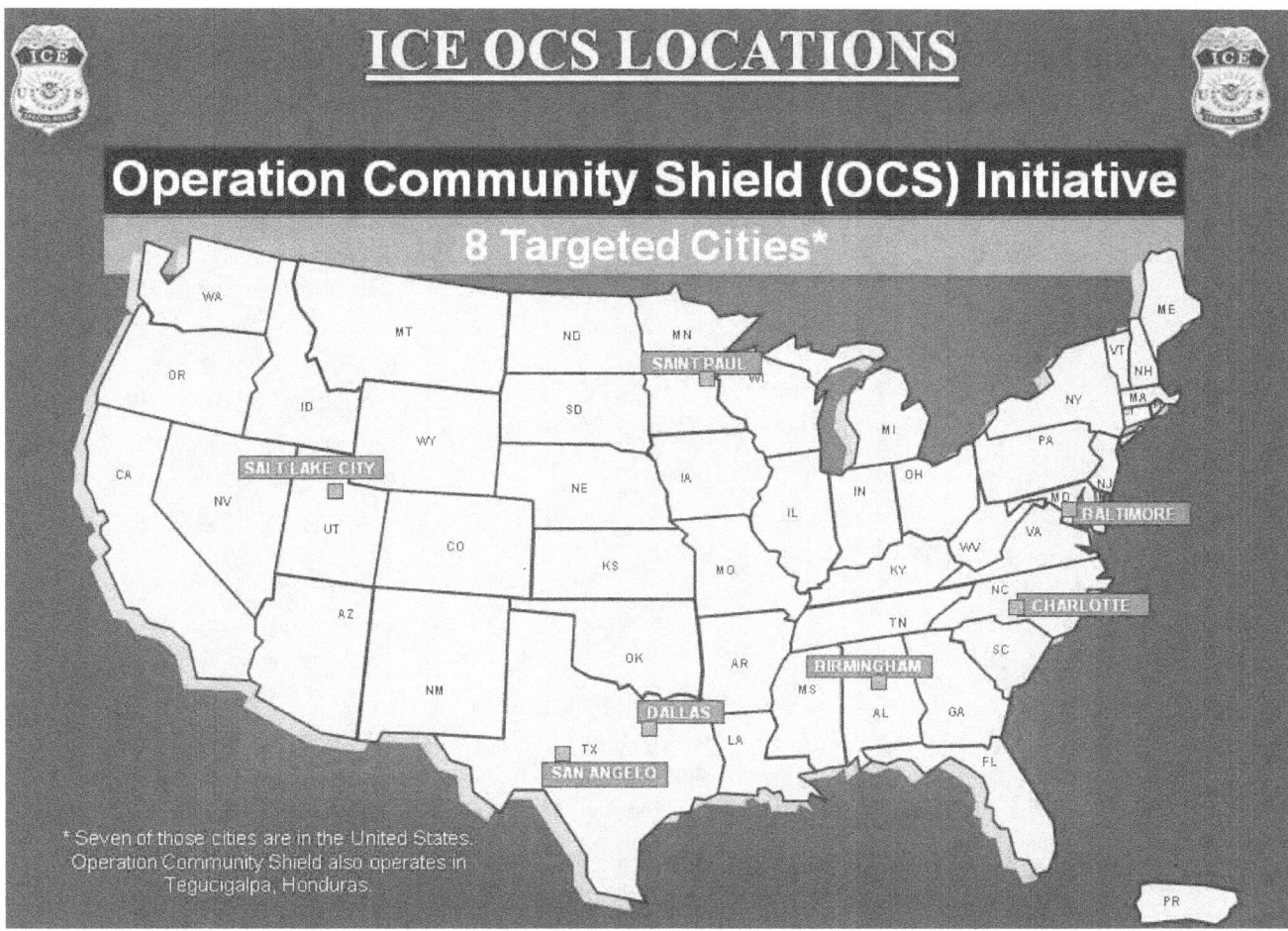

Source: ICE

APPENDIX D.
Acknowledgements

FEDERAL
US Department of Defense
Naval Criminal Investigative Service
US Army
Fort Dix Criminal Investigative Division
Directorate Emergency Services USAG-HI
US Department of Homeland Security
US Border Patrol
US Citizenship and Immigration Services
US Customs and Border Protection
US Homeland Security Investigations
US Department of the Interior
Bureau of Land Management
US Department of Justice
Bureau of Alcohol, Tobacco, Firearms and Explosives
Drug Enforcement Administration
Federal Bureau of Investigation
Federal Bureau of Prisons
Immigration and Customs Enforcement
National Drug Intelligence Center
National Gang Center
National Gang Intelligence Center
US Marshals Service
US Probation and Parole
US Department of State

LOCAL, STATE, AND REGIONAL

ALABAMA
Alabama Fusion Center
Bessemer Police Department
Birmingham Police Department
Etowah County Drug Task Force
Irondale Police Department
Madison County Sheriff's Office
Pelham Police Department

ALASKA
Alaska Department of Corrections
Anchorage Police Department

ARIZONA
Arizona Adult Probation
Arizona Department of Corrections
Arizona Department of Juvenile Corrections
Arizona Department of Public Safety
Arizona DPS-State Gang Task Force (GIITEM) Central District
Arizona State Prison Kingman / MTC
Cottonwood Police Department
Lake Havasu City Police Department
Maricopa County Sheriff's Office
Phoenix Police Department
Rocky Mountain Information Network
Scottsdale Police Department
Tempe Police Department
Tucson Police Department

ARKANSAS
13th Judicial District Deputy Prosecutors Office
Scott County Sheriff's Office

CALIFORNIA
Alameda County Sheriff's Office
Bakersfield Police Department
Bear Valley Police Department
Berkeley Police Department
Baldwin Park School Police Department
California Department of Corrections and Rehabilitation
California Highway Patrol
Chula Vista Police Department
Coachella Valley Gang Task Force
Compton School Police Department
Concord Police Department
Corona Police Department
Delano Community Correctional Facility
Eureka Police Department
Exeter Police Department
Fresno County Sheriff's Office
Garden Grove Police Department
Gilroy Police Department
Greenfield Police Department
Hollister Police Department
Huntington Beach Police Department
Inglewood Police Department
Kern County Sheriff's Office
Los Angeles Police Department
Lincoln Police Department
Long Beach Police Department
Los Angeles County District Attorney
Los Angeles County Probation Department
Los Angeles County Sheriff's Department
Marina Police Department
Merced Multi-Agency Gang Task Force

Montebello Police Department

Monterey County Probation Department

Monterey Police Department

Morgan Hill Police Department

Mountain View Police Department

Napa County Probation Department

National City Police Department

Oakland Police Department

Office of the Fresno County District Attorney

Oxnard Police Department

Pacific Grove Police Department

Pittsburg Police Department

Placer County District Attorney's Office

Riverside County District Attorney's Office

Riverside Sheriff's Department

Sacramento County Sheriff's Department

Sacramento Police Department

San Benito County Probation Department

San Benito County Sheriff's Office

San Bernardino County Sheriff's Department

San Diego County Probation Department

San Diego Police Department

San Leandro Police Department

San Luis Obispo County Sheriff's Department

Sanger Police Department

Santa Ana Police Department

Santa Barbara County Sheriff

Santa Barbara Police Department

Santa Barbara Sheriff's Department

Santa Clara County Probation Department

Santa Monica Police Department

San Bernardino County Sheriff's Department

San Diego Sheriff's Department

Simi Valley Police Department

Sonoma County Sheriff's Office

South Gate Police Department

Southern Alameda County Major Crime Task Force

Stockton Police Department

Tehachapi Police Department

Tuolumne County Sheriff

Ukiah Police Department

Vallejo Police Department

Ventura Police Department

West Covina Police Department

West Sacramento Police Department

Whittier Police Department

COLORADO

10th Judicial District Probation Department

Aurora Police Department

Colorado Department of Corrections

Garfield County Sheriff's Office

Greeley Police Department

Mesa County Sheriff's Office

Thornton Police Department

CONNECTICUT

Connecticut State Police

Danbury Police Department

Meriden Police Department

New Haven Police Department

South Windsor Police Department

West Hartford Police Department

DELAWARE

Delaware State Police

New Castle County Police

Wilmington Police Department

DISTRICT OF COLUMBIA

US Attorney's Office

Washington DC Metropolitan Police Department

FLORIDA

Alachua County Sheriff's Office

Central Florida Intelligence Exchange

Florida Department of Corrections

Florida Department of Law Enforcement

Fort Myers Police Department

Hernando County Sheriff's Office

Highlands County Sheriff's Office

Hillsborough County Sheriff

Jacksonville Sheriff's Office

Lake County Sheriff's Office

Lee County Sheriff's Office

Maitland Police Department

Marion County Sheriff's Office

Martin County Sheriff's Office

Miami-Dade Corrections & Rehabilitations

Ocala Police Department

Okeechobee County Sheriff's Office

Orange County Corrections

Orange County Sheriff's Office

Orlando Police Department

Oviedo Police Department

Polk County Sheriff's Office

Sanford Police Department

Sarasota Sheriff's Office

Seminole County Sheriff's Office

Tallahassee Police Department

Seminole Police Department

Titusville Police Department

Volusia County Sheriff's Office

GEORGIA

Cobb County Sheriff's Office

Douglasville Police Department

Georgia Bureau of Investigation

Gwinnett County Police Department

LaGrange Police Department

Richmond County Board of
Education Public Safety

Spalding County Sheriff's Office

ILLINOIS

Bensenville Police Department

Bloomington Police Department

Chicago Police Department

Decatur Police Department

Dolton Police Department

DuPage County State's Attorney's
Office

Hanover Park Police Department

Illinois Department of Corrections

Jo Daviess County Sheriff's Office

Lake County Sheriff Department

Schaumburg Police Department

INDIANA

Anderson Police Department

Boone County Sheriff Department

Cumberland Police Department

Elkhart County Sheriff's Office

Evansville Police Department

Indiana Department of Corrections

Parke County Sheriff's Office

Pendleton Correctional Facility

Richmond Police Department

Southwest Indiana Violent Crime
Task Force

IOWA

Dubuque Police Department

Iowa Department of Corrections

Jasper County Sheriff's Office

Storm Lake Police Department

Warren County Sheriff's Office

KANSAS

Kansas Bureau of Investigation

Lawrence Police Department

Topeka Police Department

Wichita Police Department

KENTUCKY

Henderson Police Department

Kentucky Department of Juvenile
Justice

Louisville Metro Police Department

McCracken County Regional Jail

LOUISIANA

Alexandria Police Narcotics Division

Creola Police Department

Denham Springs Police Department

Grant Parish Constable

Grant Parish Sheriff's Office

Iberia Parish Sheriff's Office

Jefferson Parish Sheriff's Office

Louisiana Department of Corrections

Louisiana State Police

Metro Narcotics of Ouachita

New Orleans Police Department

Office of Juvenile Justice

MAINE

Lewiston Police Department

MARYLAND

Anne Arundel County Police
Department

Calvert County Sheriff's Office

Charles County Sheriff's Office

Greenbelt City Police Department

Hagerstown Department of Police

Harford County Sheriff's Office

Maryland Coordination and Analysis
Center

Maryland Department of Corrections

Montgomery County Police

Prince George's County Police
Department

Wicomico County Department of
Corrections

MASSACHUSETTS

Boston Police Department

Chicopee Police Department

Fitchburg Police Department

Hampden County Sheriff's
Department

Haverhill Police Department

Holyoke Police Department

Lowell Police Department

Massachusetts State Police

Springfield Police Department

Worcester Police Department

MICHIGAN

Benton Township Police Department

Berrien County Sheriff's Department

Escanaba Public Safety Department

Grand Rapids Police Department

Holland Police Department

Muskegon Police Department

Oakland County Violent Gang Task
Force

Ottawa County Sheriff's Office

Unadilla Township Police
Department

West Michigan Enforcement Team

MINNESOTA

Dakota County Community
Corrections

Minneapolis Police Department

Owatonna Police Department

Prairie Island Tribal Police

Saint Peter Police Department

Shakopee Police Department

MISSISSIPPI

Gulf Coast Regional Fugitive Task
Force

Gulfport Police Department

Magee Police Department

Narcotics Task Force of Jackson
County

US Attorney's Office, Southern
District of Mississippi

MISSOURI

Berkeley Police Department

Joplin Police Department

Kansas City Missouri Police
Department

Missouri Department of Corrections

Monett Police Department

Saint Louis County Police
Department

St. Charles Police Department

St. Joseph Missouri Police
Department

St. Louis County Police Department

St. Louis Metropolitan Police
Department

MONTANA

Crossroads Correctional Center

Laurel Police Department

Missoula Police Department

Montana Department of Corrections

NEBRASKA

Bellevue Police Department

City of Gering Police Department

Columbus Police Department

Crete Police Department

Grand Island Police Department

Kearney Police Department

Omaha Police Department

NEVADA

Las Vegas Metropolitan Police
Department

Washoe County Sheriff's Office

NEW HAMPSHIRE

Belknap County Sheriff's Department

Concord Police Department

Keene Police Department

Manchester Police Department

Manchester Weed and Seed
Program

Merrimack County Department of
Corrections

Nashua Police Department

Somersworth Police Department

NEW JERSEY

Bound Brook Police Department

Essex County Prosecutor's Office

Kenilworth Police Department

Linden Police Department

Passaic County Sheriff's Department

NEW MEXICO

Albuquerque Police Department

Catron County Sheriff's Department

Eddy County Sheriff's Office

Pueblo of Acoma Police Department

NEW YORK

Dutchess County Sheriff's Office

Glens Falls Police Department

Nassau County Police Department

NORTH CAROLINA

Duplin County Sheriff's Office

Durham Police Department

Fayetteville Police Department

Gastonia Police Department

New Hanover County Sheriff

North Carolina Department of
Corrections

Shelby Police Department

Wake Forest Police Department

NORTH DAKOTA

Heart of America Correctional and
Treatment Center

North Dakota Department of
Corrections

OHIO

Akron Police Department

Canton Police Department

Columbus, Ohio Division of Police

Dayton Police Department

Lake Metroparks Ranger Department

Montpelier Police Department

Springfield Ohio Division of Police

OKLAHOMA

Davis Correctional Facility

Eastern Shawnee Tribal Police

North Fork Correctional facility

Oklahoma City Police Department

Oklahoma Department of
Corrections

Owasso Police Department

OREGON

Crook County Sheriff's Office

Portland Police Bureau

PENNSYLVANIA

California University of Pennsylvania Police Department

Cumberland County Prison

Ephrata Police Department

Lackawanna County District Attorney

Lackawanna County Prison

Lancaster County District Attorney

Manheim Borough Police Department

Mifflin County Regional Police Department

Montgomery County Adult Probation & Parole Department

Pennsylvania Capitol Police

Pennsylvania State Police

Philadelphia-Camden HIDTA

Slippery Rock University Police

PUERTO RICO

Metropolitan Detention Center, Guaynabo

Police of Puerto Rico

RHODE ISLAND

Providence Police Department

Rhode Island Department of Corrections

SOUTH CAROLINA

Anderson County Gang Task Force

Bamberg Police Department

Charleston County Sheriff Office

Chester City Police Department

Colleton County Sheriff's Office

Columbia Police Department

Darlington County Sheriff's Office

Darlington Police Department

Dorchester County Sheriff's Office

Florence County Sheriff's Office

Florence Police Department

Fountain Inn Police Department

Greenwood County Sheriff's Office

Greenwood Police Department

Greer Police Department

Hampton County Sheriff Office

Hartsville Police Department

Lancaster City Police Department

Lancaster Police Department

Latta Police Department

Lexington Medical Health Services – Public Safety

Palmetto Protection Agency, Inc.

Prosperity Police Department

Rock Hill Police Department

South Carolina Department of Corrections

Spartanburg Public Safety Department

Summerville Police Department

Timmonsville Police Department

West Columbia Police Department

SOUTH DAKOTA

Rapid City Police Department

Tripp County Sheriff's Office

TENNESSEE

Bradley County Juvenile Detention

Chattanooga Police Department

Coffee County Sheriff's Department

Columbia Police Department

Cookeville Police Department

Covington Police Department

Fayette County Sheriff's Department

Franklin Police Department

Hardeman County Correctional Facility

Juvenile Court of Jefferson County

Knoxville Police Department

Metro Nashville Police Department

Oak Ridge Police Department

Rutherford County Sheriff's Department

Sumner County Sheriff's Office

Tennessee Bureau of Investigation

Tennessee Department of Correction

TEXAS

Amarillo Police Department

Andrews Department of Public Safety

Austin Police Department

Bastrop County Sheriff's Office

Baytown Police Department

Bexar County Fire Marshal's Office

Bosque County Sheriff's Office

Collin County District Attorney's Office

Dallas ISD Police & Security

Dallas Police Department Gang Unit

Donna ISD Police Department

El Paso County Sheriff's Office

Harlingen Police Department

Hays County Juvenile Probation

Hidalgo County Constable – Pct 3

Hidalgo County District Attorney's Office

Hidalgo County Sheriff's Office

Hutchinson County Sheriff's Office

Kenedy County Sheriff Office

Luling Police Department

Maverick County Detention Center

Nacogdoches Police Department

New Caney ISD Police Department

Reagan County Sheriff's Office

San Antonio Police Department

San Marcos Police Department

Schertz Police Department

Texas Alcoholic Beverage Commission

Texas Department of Criminal Justice

Travis County Sheriff's Office

Texas Department of Public Safety

University of Texas Health Science Center Police

UTAH

West Valley City Police Department

VERMONT

No reporting

VIRGINIA

Abingdon Police Department

Alexandria Police Department

Alexandria Sheriff's Office

Arlington County Police Department

Bland Correctional Center

Chesapeake Police Department

Chesterfield County Police Department

Chincoteague Police Department

City of Chesapeake Police Department

City of Harrisonburg Police Department

City of Manassas Police Department

Department of Conservation and Recreation

Department of Juvenile Justice

Fairfax County Police Department

Hampton Police Division

Newport News Police Department

Norfolk Police Division

Prince William County Police Department

Richmond Police Department

Staunton Police Department

Suffolk Police Department

Town of Herndon Police Department

Town of Vienna Police Department

Virginia Department of Corrections

Virginia Correctional Center for Women

Virginia Port Authority Police Department

Virginia State Police

Warsaw Probation and Parole Office

WASHINGTON

Everson Police Department

King County Jail

King County Sheriff's Office

Lynnwood Police Department

Nisqually Indian Tribe

Northwest High Intensity Drug Trafficking Area

Seattle Police Department

Washington State Department of Corrections

WEST VIRGINIA

Eastern Panhandle Potomac Highlands SSTF

Martinsburg Police Department

Philippi Police Department

WISCONSON

Lac Courte Oreilles Tribal Police

Milwaukee Police Department

Wisconsin Department of Corrections

WYOMING

Wyoming Highway Patrol

Endnotes

[1] US Department of Justice (USDOJ); "Highlights of the 2009 National Youth Gang Survey;" Office of Juvenile Justice and Delinquency Prevention; National Gang Center; May 2011.

[2] Open Source News Release; "11 Alleged MS-13 Members Indicted on Racketeering and Other Charges in a Series of Violent Crimes; ICE; 4 May 2011. Open Source Article; "Officials Concerned About Gang Violence in Prince George's County;" *Washington Examiner*; available at www.washingtonexaminer.com.

[3] USDOJ; "Federal Racketeering Indictment Leads to Arrest of 8 Members, Associates of San Gabriel Valley Street Gang;" Press Release; 8 June 2010; available at www.justice.gov/usao/cac/pressroom/pr/2010/091.html.

[4] USDOJ; "National Drug Threat Assessment 2010;" National Drug Intelligence Center; February 2010.

[5] NAGIA Quick Guide to Gangs, National Alliance of Gang Investigators Association; April 2010.

[6] Open Source News Article; "Tips for dealing with Asian Gangs;" Police One; 21 May 2009; available at www.Policeone.com.

[7] USDOJ; *National Drug Threat Assessment 2010*; NDIC; February 2010. Open Source News Article, "Pot houses linked to gangs, marijuana dispensaries;" *Whittier Daily* News; 6 September 2010; available at www.Whittierdailynews.com. Open Source News Article, "Asian Pot Ring Busted, Noted Restaurateur Suspect;" CBS4 Denver; 7 March 2010; available at www.CBS4denver.com.

[8] Open Source News Article; "Somali Gangs Ran Sex Ring in 3 US States, Authorities Say;" *Fox News*; 8 November 2010; available at www.foxnews.com.

[9] Online news article; "Judge sets $2 million bond in alleged murder, robbery;" *Ohio Post*; 15 April 2009.

[10] FBI Indianapolis Division; "Twenty-Two Charged Federally in Evansville Drug Trafficking Case;" Press Release; 4 February 2010; available at http://indianapolis.fbi.gov/dojpressrel/pressrel10/ip020410.htm.

[11] NAGIA Quick Guide to Gangs; National Alliance of Gang Investigators Association; April 2010.

[12] Open Source News Article; "Hybrid Gangs responsible for rise in North Las Vegas Crime," 13 *Action News Las Vegas*; 25 July 2010; available at http://www.ktnv.com/Global/story.asp;13.

[13] Open Source News Article; "Man charged with shooting couple on Maple Valley Trail"; *The Seattle Times*; 3 January 2011; available at http://seattletimes.nwsource.com/html/theblotter/2013837934_man_charged_with_xx_in_connect.html.

[14] Open Source News Article; "Teen gets probation in attacks on homeless;" *Gazette-Times*; 22 January 2010; available at http://www.gazettetime.com/news/local/article_3b43539a-07ab-11df-b6ae-001cc4c03286.html.

[15] US Immigration Customs Enforcement (ICE); "8 Arrested as ICE Dismantles Alien Smuggling Ring Linked to Notorious Local Street Gang;" News Release; 14 October 2009; available at www.ice.gov/news/releases/0910/091014losangeles.htm.

[16] Open Source Website; Human Smuggling and Trafficking Center (HSTC) Charter and Amendments; available at www.state.gov/m/ds/hstcenter/41444.htm.

[17] DHS; "29 Charged with Sex Trafficking Juveniles;" ICE; News Release; 8 November 2010; available at www.ice.gov/news/releases/1011/101108nashville.htm.

[18] Open News Source Article; "Report Links Street Gangs to Child Prostitution;" KPBS News; 23 November 2010; available at www.kpbs.org/news/2010/nov/09/report-links-street-gangs-child-prostitution.

[19] Open Source News Article; Kevin Johnson; *USA Today*; "Drug Cartels Unite Rival Gangs to Work for Common Bad;" *USA Today*; 16 March 2010.

[20] USDOJ; "National Drug Threat Assessment 2010;" National Drug Intelligence Center; February 2010.

[21] USDOJ; "National Drug Threat Assessment 2010;" National Drug Intelligence Center; February 2010.

[22] Open Source News Article; "Drug Cartels Uniting Rival Gangs;" *USA Today*; 3 March 2010; available at www.usatoday.com.

[23] USDOJ; "National Drug Threat Assessment 2010;" National Drug Intelligence Center; February 2010.

[24] Open Source News Article; "US Mexico Drug Gangs Form Alliances;" *Washington Times*; 26 March 2010; available at www.washingtimes.com.

[25] Open Source News Article; Kevin Johnson; "Drug Cartels Unite Rival Gangs to Work for Common Bad;" USA Today; 16 March 2010; available at www.usatoday.com.

[26] Open Source News Article; "US Mexico Drug Gangs Form Alliances;" *Washington Times*; 26 March 2010; available at www.washingtontimes.com.

[27] USDOJ; "National Drug Threat Assessment 2010;" National Drug Intelligence Center; February 2010. Open Source News Article; "US Mexico Drug Gangs Form Alliances;" *Washington Times*; 26 March 2010; available at www.washingtontimes.com.

[28] Open Source News Article; "La Familia' North of the Border;" STRATFOR *Global Intelligence*; 3 December 2009; available at http://www.stratfor.com/weekly/20091203_la_familia_north_border.

[29] Open Source News Article; "New Jersey Authorities Indict 34 Lucchese Crime Family Bust from 'Operation Heat';" *New Jersey.com*; 14 May 2010.

[30] Open Source News Article; "Authorities crack down on transnational Armenian Power crime group;" *CNN*; 17 February 2011; available at www.cnn.com.

[31] Open Source News Article; "N.J. Inmate's Ordered Killing Shows Danger of Cell Phones in Prison," http://www.nj.com/news/index.ssf/2010/06/nj_state_prison_inmate_is_char.html; June 11, 2010; Online News Article; "Prosecutor: Trenton prison inmate Anthony Kidd used cell phone to order murder of girlfriend Kendra Degrasse," http://www.trentonian.com/articles/2010/06/11/news/doc4c11432d64621687151693.txt; June 12, 2010

[32] Open Source News Article; "Prisoner Ordered Hit Outside of Prison With Smuggle Cell Phone;" 13 September 2010; available at http://newsone.com/nation/associatedpress4/prisoner-ordered-hit-outside-of-prison-with-smuggled-cell-phone/.

[33] Open Source News Article; "Parole Worker Leaked Information to Gang Member;" *Fox News New York*; 1 November 2010; available at www.myfoxny.com.

[34] Open Source News Article; "Former Deputy Headed for Prison;" *PE.com*; 30 July 2010; available at www.pe.com.

[35] Open Source News Article; "Ex-Cop, James Formato, Pleads Guilty in Mob Case;" *CBS News Chicago*; 25 April 2010; available at www.thechicagosyndicate.com/2010/04/ex-cop-james-formato-pleads-guilty-in.html.

[36] Online publication; *Bureau of Justice Statistics*; Jails in Indian Country, 2008; December 2009; available at http://bjs.ojp.usdoj/index.cfm?ty=pbdetails&iid=1748.

[37] Open Source News Article; "Mexican Pot Gangs Infiltrate Indian Reservations in U.S;" *The Wall Street Journal*; 5 November 2009; available at http://online.wsj.com/article/SB125736987377028727.html.

[38] Open Source News Article; "Crunching Numbers in Mexico's Drug Conflict;" *BBC News*; 14 January 2011; available at www.bbc.com.

[39] Stratfor Global Intelligence Center; "Mexican Drug Wars: Bloodiest Year to Date;" 20 December 2010.

[40] Open Source News Article; "Napolitano: Border security better than ever;" CBS News; 25 March 2011; http://www.cbsnews.com/8301-503544_162-20047102-503544.html.

[41] USDOJ; "National Drug Threat Assessment 2010;" National Drug Intelligence Center; February 2010.

[42] USDOJ; "National Drug Threat Assessment 2010;" National Drug Intelligence Center; February 2010.

[43] Open Source News Article; "Barrio Azteca threat targets law officers;" *El Paso Times*; 25 March 2010; available at www.elpasotimes.com/ci_14753458.

[44] USDOJ; "National Drug Threat Assessment 2010;" National Drug Intelligence Center; February 2010.

[45] USDOJ; "National Drug Threat Assessment 2010;" National Drug Intelligence Center; February 2010.

[46] USDOJ; "National Drug Threat Assessment 2010;" National Drug Intelligence Center; February 2010.

[47] Press Release; "Former Marines Arrested on Weapons Charges;" USDOJ; ATF; 8 November 2010.

[48] Press Release; "Three men, US Navy Seal, Arrested for Unlawfully Trafficking in Machine Guns;" US DOJ; ATF; 4 November 2010.

[49] Open Source News Article; *MSNBC.com*, "California Gang Officers Again Targeted by Booby-Trap,"1 March 2010; available at www.msnbc.com.

[50] Investigative Consultants; email correspondence; 29 November 2010.

[51] Investigative Consultants; email correspondence; 29 November 2010. Superior Court of the State of California, County of Los Angeles, Central District; *First Amended Complaint for Injunction and Civil Penalties*; 15 March 2010.

[52] Open Source News Article; "Seeing Green;" *Baltimore City Paper*; 11 August 2010; available at www.citypaper.com.

[53] Open Source News Article; "Two Dozen Charged in Alleged Gang-led Mortgage Fraud;" *Reuters News*; 7 April 2009; available at www.reuters.com.

[54] Open Source News Article; "Border Crime Sweep Nets Drugs, 246 Arrests;" *Sign On San Diego*; 28 March 2011; available at www.signonsandiego.com.

[55] FBI; "Violent Border Gang Indicted; Members Charged in Consulate Murders;" News Release; 9 March 2011; available at www.fbi.gov.

[56] FBI; "Forty-One Gang Members and Associates in Five Districts Charged with Crimes Including Racketeering, Murder, Drug Trafficking, and Firearms Trafficking;" *News Release*; 9 February 2011; available at www.fbi.gov.